Subject	LC	Decimal
Physical Geography	GB	551
Oceanography	GC	551.46
Anthropology	GN	572
Folklore	GR	398
Manners & Customs	GT	390
Sports, Games, Recreation	GV	790
Social Sciences	H	300
Statistics	HA	310
Economics	HB–HJ	330
Labor	HD	331
Commerce	HF	380
Finance	HG	332
Sociology	HN–HX	300
Political Science	J	320, 350
United States	JK	353
Europe	JN	354
International Law	JX	341
Law	K	340
Education	L	370
History of Education	LA	370
Theory & Practice	LB	371
Universities (U.S.)	LD	378
Music	M	780
Fine Arts	N	700
Architecture	NA	720
Sculpture	NB	730
Graphic Arts	NC	740
Painting	ND	750
Language	P	400
French	PC	440
Spanish	PC	460
Italian	PC	450
English	PE	420
German	PF	430
Oriental	PJ	495
Literature	P	800
Classical	PA	870–880
Oriental	PL	895
General	PN	800–809
French	PQ	840
Italian	PQ	850
Spanish	PQ	860
English	PR	820

continued on back end papers

Research

Research
A Practical Guide to
Finding Information

Peter Fenner
Martha C. Armstrong

William Kaufmann, Inc.
Los Altos, California

To Don, whose encouragement and support made my
dreams possible.

—MCA

To KTL, with PB, and three F's—TA, BA, AR—who
render my dreams worthwhile.

—PF

Library of Congress Cataloging in Publication Data

Fenner, Peter, 1937–
  Research: a practical guide to finding information.

  Bibliography: p. 192
  Includes index.
  1. Research—Methodology—Handbooks, manuals, etc.   2. Libraries—
Handbooks, manuals, etc.
I. Armstrong, Martha, 1923–   joint author
II. Title.
Q180.55.M4F46   001.4'2   81-4589
ISBN 0-86576-010-1   AACR2

10   9   8   7   6   5   4   3   2
Printed in the United States of America

Contents

Preface

Research will help you find information—public or private, published or unpublished. By design it can be used either independently or in formal courses of study such as college-level basic skills classes. For best results, most readers should follow the sequence of chapters, completing all the exercises as they go. Students working independently will profit from the help of a knowledgeable critic (librarian, teacher, scientist, or other advisor) when the time comes to evaluate performance on the exercises.

The search strategies and techniques we have offered here are applicable to all fields of study, but our examples and references focus on the literature of science and technology where accumulated knowledge and data are so vital to continuing progress. Researchers in other fields may find it helpful to add relevant reference titles to the listings we've provided; appropriate catalog subdivisions might also be added to the endpapers.

Of all the people involved in the development of this book, perhaps the most helpful have been the hundreds of students who, since 1973, have answered questionnaires about earlier versions of *Research*. Their detailed and candid comments have been invaluable. Two former colleagues at Governors State University were also especially helpful. T. David Ainsworth, an instructional designer *par excellence*, kept asking the kinds of basic questions students would ask—often the important but elementary ones that neither of us wanted to think about—forcing us to assess critically our purpose and product. Richard Pollak, armed with expertise in computer-assisted instruction and learning theory, wisely dissuaded us from our early intention to depend on the computer, encouraging us simply to ask single questions, one at a time. Their efforts have made *Research* a much better tool than it would otherwise have been. Finally, the patience and forbearance of our families and friends have been essential during our years of progress on this project.

David Mike Hamilton and other members of the staff of William Kaufmann, Inc. have been of inestimable help as the work was transformed from final draft to finished book. Richard Burke's editorial incisiveness and copy-editing skills helped to fine-tune the manuscript; and we are all indebted to Sidney Harris, whose drawings here and elsewhere help readers to remember the worth of levity in weighty matters.

To all of you, our warmest thanks.

Peter Fenner
Martha C. Armstrong
Park Forest South

Using the Card Catalog 1

INTRODUCTION

Research is for people who have previous skills in using a library and for those who don't. **This chapter will help you review or learn card catalog use.** Working your way through the tests that conclude this and the following chapter should tell you whether you are ready to skip ahead to Chapter Three.

To go beyond the scope of *Research*, first consult our sources; they are cited throughout this book. If they are unavailable in your library, ask your librarian about obtaining them through an inter-library loan.

Here are some titles; are they in the alphabetical sequence used in *your* library?

I met a man
Image of Africa
In case of fire
Indonesia
In the days of giants
The Inca
Indelicate hors d'oeuvres
The ants
Thanks, but no thanks!
Theatrical apparatus reviewed
Then: anthills!

There are likely fewer errors in that ordering than you might first suspect. In our library, two of these titles would be out of place. Before leaving this chapter, you should be able to arrange these titles according to the filing rules of the library where you will do most of your research. You should know your library's filing conventions for cards representing works in the stacks, in storage, or in special collections. You should also be acquainted with your library's special holdings and with the librarians' specialized subject-matter skills. Moreover, you should be able to find reference works at any desired level of generalization or specificity.

Should you want more information on the materials presented here, review the source documents we used in preparing this chapter:

Kirk, Jr., Thomas G., 1978, *Library research guide to biology*, Ann Arbor, Pierian Press, pp. 8–12

Lasworth, E. J., 1972, *Reference sources in science and technology*, Metuchen, Scarecrow Press, pp. ix–xi, 1–2

Seely, Pauline, A., 1968, *A.L.A. rules for filing catalog cards*, 2nd ed., Chicago, 260 pp.

THE MAIN CARD CATALOG

Libraries sometimes have several card catalogs, all but one of them relatively small and specialized. Virtually all libraries use one *main* card catalog.

As you prepare to work with the main card catalog in your library, understand that it usually indexes only the general subjects of books, rarely their component parts. Also, while it does list authors, titles, and often the subject matter of books, and while it may list journal titles, the catalog does not provide access to individual periodical articles. And as the main catalog does not attempt to evaluate books listed, there is no substitute for actually studying a book for possible use.

The main card catalog, then, is a record of all the circulating and reference books and other materials in a library. Cards in the main catalog carry three kinds of headings: author, title, and subject headings. Main catalogs are often divided into two sections. Many libraries, however, have combined both the author-title and subject sections of the catalog into a single alphabetical sequence (a "dictionary catalog"—see below).

AUTHOR-TITLE CATALOG

This is the catalog you'll use to find the call number of a book whose author or title you know. The author-heading card is the main entry. It is likely to contain more extensive information about the book in question than would the title- or subject-heading cards.

If the author's name is not known, books may be located by looking up the title, which is typed above the author's name at the top of the catalog card. Titles of books are usually listed, particularly if the author is anonymous. Some libraries do not list all the titles beginning with phrases such as *History of, Outline of, Report on.*

In a dictionary catalog, i.e., an undivided card catalog, all types of entries are interfiled: author, title, and subject cards are arranged in a single alphabet. The sequence of those entries, for an identical work, varies according to filing conventions adhered to in any particular library (see Figure 1).

Filing conventions given below suggest some of the rules to be aware of when you try to locate a card. They are typical for medium-sized to large libraries.

```
          LINCOLN, ABRAHAM, PRES. U.S., 1809-1865--
E           ICONOGRAPHY.
457.92    Lincoln, Abraham, Pres. U. S., 1809–1865.
1965         Lincoln ; his words and his world [compiled] by the editors
          of Country beautiful magazine. Editorial direction: Mi-
          chael P. Dineen.  Edited by Robert L. Polley.  [1st ed.]
          Waukesha, Wis., Published by Country Beautiful Founda-
          tion for Hawthorn Books, New York [1965]
              98 p.  illus (part col.)  facsims. (part col.)  ports. (part col.)
```

```
             Lincoln
E
457.92    Lincoln, Abraham, Pres. U. S., 1809–1865.
1965         Lincoln ; his words and his world [compiled] by the editors
          of Country beautiful magazine.  Editorial direction: Mi-
          chael P. Dineen.  Edited by Robert L. Polley.  [1st ed.]
          Waukesha, Wis., Published by Country Beautiful Founda-
          tion for Hawthorn Books, New York [1965]
              98 p.  illus (part col.)  facsims. (part col.)  ports. (part col.)
              89 cm.
```

```
E
457.92    Lincoln, Abraham, Pres. U. S., 1809–1865.
1965         Lincoln ; his words and his world [compiled] by the editors
          of Country beautiful magazine.  Editorial direction: Mi-
          chael P. Dineen.  Edited by Robert L. Polley.  [1st ed.]
          Waukesha, Wis., Published by Country Beautiful Founda-
          tion for Hawthorn Books, New York [1965]
              98 p.  illus (part col.)  facsims. (part col.)  ports. (part col.)
              32 cm.


              1. Lincoln, Abraham, Pres. U. S., 1809–1865—Iconography.
          I. Polley, Robert L., ed.  II. Country beautiful.  III. Title.

          E457.92  1965            923.173            65—12399

          Library of Congress        [66f7]
```

Figure 1. Here are author, title, and subject cards for one work. Between the first two would be filed cards for other works written by this Lincoln and by other Lincolns (with first names after Abraham. . .). Between the second and third cards would be cards for other works entitled Lincoln. Around the third card would be cards about other Lincoln-related subjects. Using the very latest Library of Congress filing rules, the second-shown card, above, would be filed first, because Lincoln stands alone.

FILING CONVENTIONS

The following outline will not necessarily explain all of the conventions used in your library; don't hesitate to ask your librarian to show you the filing rules used there.

1. In a two-section main card catalog, subjects (subject-added entries) are filed in one section. Authors and titles (main entry, and additional or later edition information placed above the main entry, e.g., author-added, title-added, and series-added entries) are interfiled in the other section.

2. The arrangement of the catalog cards in the author-title catalog is alphabetical (see the exceptions listed below, e.g., a chronological or numerical arrangement is used in certain cases for clarity). Punctuation marks are disregarded in filing. Examples:

    New Republic
    New York (City) Zoological Park
    New York Ermines
    New York Times
    New Yorker Magazine
    Newsweek

3. Filing is chronological in cases of:

    a. Subject headings involving history and historical subdivisions. This includes historical periods, even if they have no date listed. For example, *U.S. History, American Revolution*, is filed:

        U.S.—History—1776

    Filing is in order of the first date given, with the earliest coming first. Periods that have the same beginning date are filed in order, with the longest period coming first. Thus:

        U.S.—History—1945–
        U.S.—History—1945–1960
        U.S.—History—1945–1947
        U.S.—History—1950–

    If alphabetical and historical headings and subheadings are present, the historical headings are filed first, then historical sub-headings, then alphabetical headings and alphabetical sub-headings, all under the same main heading.

    b. Multiple editions of the same book or other materials are filed in order of number, with the first edition filed first.

    c. Dated series are filed under the series title, in order of the dates, and with the earliest dates first. When a date is used in a title, it is arranged according to the full spelling of the common pronunciation of the date: for *1984*, read: *nineteen eighty-four*; for *101*, read: *one hundred one*. However, when similar titles with different dates signify historical sequences, they are filed chronologically. Also, titles that are part of an apparent historical sequence involving different dates and locations (e.g., *Olympics: Lake Placid, 1980*) are arranged by the first part of the title; if the location appears before the date in such a title, the two are inverted for filing purposes:

  Olympics: 1976, Innsbruck
  Olympics: 1980, Lake Placid

4. Alphabetical filing is letter-by-letter. Library alphabetization considers a space between words as a letter that precedes an *a*, thus:

 Free Song
 Freedom

Apostrophes, quotation marks, and any modifications to letters are ignored, and a hyphen or dash is considered to be a space unless a prefix or suffix is involved. (See rules 13 and 16.)

5. Filing ignores:

 a. the initial articles *a*, *an*, *the*, and their equivalents in foreign languages, except when they are part of a proper name. Common foreign articles that are, thus, dropped from the filing sequence when they occur at the beginning of a title, include:

Das	Die	Eit	Gli	Las	s
De	Een	El	Het	Le	't
Dei	Eene	En	I	Les	Un
Den	Ei	Et	Il	Lo	Un'
Der	Ein	Ett	L'	Los	Una
Det	Eine	Gl'	La	'n	Une

 b. punctuation, except that personal surname entries are arranged before other entries beginning with the same word or combination of words. Examples of titles alphabetized:

 Mr. W. Thomas
 Mrs. Walter Thomas
 Thomas' Storied Fortune
 Walter Thomas
 The Walter Thomas Story

6. Filing continues alphabetically even if the author or title entry is longer than a single line.

   a. Cards having identical subjects are then arranged according to the second line or entry, using the same set of rules.

   b. Under a given author's name, cards are filed alphabetically according to title, disregarding any second authors listed. If these titles are alphabetically similar, shorter ones precede longer ones. Authors with the same last name are arranged alphabetically by their first names. Authors are usually individuals, but may be companies, agencies, or other organizations, such as:

      American Chemical Society
      Massachusetts Institute of Technology
      Society for Experimental Biology (Gt. Brt.)
      U.S. Department of Commerce
      U.S. Department of Health, Education, and Welfare

7. Single letters or initials are filed before a word beginning with the same letter, such as:

   ABC of technology
   A. B. Czerny lectures in geochemistry
   Aaron, Robert

   Initials, thus, are treated as one-letter words. These include initials representing names of organizations that are usually known by their initials. *International Business Machines*, for example, would be filed:

   IBM

   In these cases, one cross-reference card is filed under the full name and a second cross-reference card is filed under the initialized form.

   The exception to this rule involves acronyms, which are abbreviations or initial letters of a group of words generally written and spoken as a single word, such as:

FORTRAN	(for *FOR*mula in *TRAN*slation)
NATO	(for *N*orth *A*tlantic *T*reaty *O*rganization)
UNESCO	(for *U*nited *N*ations *E*conomic and *S*ocial *CO*uncil)

   Acronyms are filed as words, rather than initials; but they also receive cross-reference cards filed under the full name and under the one-letter-word rule for initials, as an aid to those not aware of the general filing rules.

8. Abbreviations appear on the cards as abbreviations, if so used on the original works, but they are, with one exception, filed as if the abbreviations were spelled out. For example:

    Dr. is filed as if it were *Doctor*

    Mr. is filed as if it were *Mister*

    St. is filed as if it were *Saint*

    U.S. is filed as if it were *United States*

    USSR is filed as if it were *Union of Soviet Socialist Republics*

    The exception to this rule is the abbreviation *Mrs.*, which is filed as it is written.

    When *Mrs.* and *Sir* are followed by another name, they are filed as though written in an inverted form, thus:

    Smith, John

    Smith, Mrs. John (i.e., as if it were *Smith, John Mrs.*)

    Smith, John, pseud.

    Smith, Sir John (i.e., as if it were *Smith, John Sir*)

    Smith, Mrs.

    Smith, Samuel

9. Titles and compound names follow single surnames. Examples:

    Smith, Zachary

    Smith College Journal

    Smith-Jones, Ivy

    Smith of the Gazette

10. Elisions, contractions, and possessives are arranged as written, and as a single word. Missing words are not supplied.

11. Signs, symbols, and numbers, except those following rule 3, are arranged as if they were spelled out in the language of the entry:

    XV is filed as *fifteen*, or *fifteenth*, depending on context;

    410 is filed as *four hundred and ten*.

12. Words having more than one spelling are filed under the preferred spelling, and a cross-reference card may be filed under alternate spellings:

    Color and *Colour*

    Musical terms are filed under the singular spelling of the term:

    concerto is filed as *Concerto*

    concertos is filed under *Concerto*

    concerti is filed under *Concerto*

13. Hyphenated words are arranged as separate words when the parts can stand alone as complete words. This does not include those prefixes that indicate the name of a country or people such as:
    Anglo-
    Franco-
    Greco-

14. Compound proper names of two or more words are arranged as separate words (even if they are hyphenated) excepting those involving prefixes such as:
    De   La
    Del   O'
    El   Van

15. *M'*, *Mc*, and *Mac* in names are all treated as the prefix *Mac*, thus:
    McCabe
    MacDonald
    Machine
    M'Mahon
    McPeters
    Madness

16. Umlauts are filed as if spelled with the vowel followed by an *e*:
    ä is filed as *ae*
    ö is filed as *oe*
    ü is filed as *ue*

17. Author-added and main author entries are filed disregarding descriptive appelations such as:
    editor
    illustrator
    joint composer

18. Dates that follow the name of a person or organization and are descriptive, rather than indicative of historical placement or sequence, are filed together with those lacking such a description. (See Figure 2.)

19. Bible entries are arranged in this sequence:
    whole *Bible*
    New Testament, whole
    New Testament, individual books, alphabetically arranged
    Old Testament, whole
    Old Testament, individual books, alphabetically arranged
    Bible, as the first word of a title

```
Art Lib.
NK
1510      Anderson, Donald M
.A63          Elements of design. New York, Holt, Rinehart and
          Winston [1961]
              218 p.  Illus.  22 x 27 cm.
```

```
          Anderson, Donald L.
HF
5635        Information analysis in management
.I45        accounting / [edited by] Donald L.
          Anderson, Donald L. Raun. Santa
          Barbara [Calif.] : Wiley, c1978.
          706 p. : ill. ; 24 cm. (Wiley/
          Hamilton series in accounting and
```

```
          Anderson, Donald K., ed.
PR
2524      Ford, John, 1586-ca. 1640.
.C5           Perkin Warbeck. Edited by Donald K. Anderson, Jr.
          Lincoln, University of Nebraska Press [1965]
              xx, 114 p.  22 cm.  (Regents Renaissance drama series)
              First published in 1634 under title: The chronicle historie of Per-
```

```
PR        Anderson, Donald K              1922-
2527          John Ford, by Donald K. Anderson,
.A5       Jr.  New York, Twayne Publishers
          [1972]
              160 p.  22 cm.  (Twayne's English
          authors series, TEAS 129)
              Bibliography: p. 149-155.
```

```
DOCS.
I L       Anderson, Donald B.
GA            [The reality of widowhood / by Donald
3         B. Anderson]. [Springfield : State of
.2:       Illinois, House of Representatives,
W 53      1977]
              10 p. ; 22 cm.
          Title taken from back cover.
          Bibliography: p. 10.


              1. Widows.   I. Illinois. General
          Assembly. House of Representatives.
          II. Title

          I PfsG   09 JUN 78     3902891    IAFAnt
```

Figure 2. This sequence of cards illustrates rule 18.

20. Works concerning one author are arranged in this manner (using Shakespeare merely as one example of an author entry):
   a. Works by Shakespeare
      1. collected works, partial or complete, in one alphabet
      2. individual works by Shakespeare in one alphabet, arranged by name of play, using the short title, such as: *Hamlet*, (not the *Tragedy of Hamlet*). Criticisms of individual works are filed directly behind the individual work being criticized.
   b. Works about Shakespeare

SUBJECT HEADING CATALOG

Begin your search for information by making a list of specific subject headings that you believe to be relevant to your goal. Then go to the Library of Congress' *Subject headings used in the dictionary catalogs of the Library of Congress* (1980, 9th ed., Washington). Listings in that book are typically the subject headings used in your library's card catalog.

Different people may label the same concept with different words. Hence the need for standardized subject headings. Though subject headings do not include all the works in a library's collections, subject headings can help:

1. show where to find books on specific subjects in the card catalog;
2. show in one place the relative extent of holdings related to one subject; and,
3. indicate through cross-references other places to look that might not otherwise have been apparent.

Begin by being as specific as possible when you look for a subject. Then consider the leads you find in the card catalog. If these are too few, then go to the next higher level of generalization in the subject headings listed; but if these are too many, go to more specialized subject headings (subheadings). Don't forget to check the author-title catalog for possible related works by authors whose useful works you have already located.

If, for example, you seek a specific subject (e.g., "mercury poisoning") and cannot find a listing in *Subject headings used in the dictionary catalogs of the Library of Congress*, try a more general subject (e.g., "water pollution"). If the more general subject is unlisted, too, then refer to a dictionary or thesaurus to find related words that might be used in the subject heading you seek.

If you already know of a book that treats your subject, consult its author-title card in the card catalog: author-title cards generally list the various subject headings to which the book is relevant.

There are many inconsistencies in the arbitrary listings used by the Library of Congress—a reflection of the patch-work way these listings have grown. Because modifications of the system are continual, you should pay especial attention to user notes and emendations both in the subject headings listings and the catalog cards.

Headings are printed in boldface, subheadings are preceded by a single dash, and second-order subheadings are preceded by double dashes. The *Subject headings* book lists many cross-references usually used in the subject heading section of a library's card catalog. For example:

Cellulose
-bacteriology (QR160)
-botany (QK898.C35)
-chemistry (QD321)
-technology (TS1145)
sa-cellophane (TP986.C4)
-cellulose industry (TS932)
-hemicellulose (QK865)
-nitrocellulose (TP276)
-pyroxlin (TP939)
-rayon (TS1788)
-wood
　− −chemistry (TA421)
xx-polysaccarides (QD321)

Note the reference codes in the foregoing list:

sa, tells you to see also the related listings shown

xx, indicates other more general listings that might be consulted

x, (which is not shown in the example above) signifies a heading that might also be applicable to the subject, but that is not authorized for use within the Library of Congress

If the term you seek is not listed, try using synonyms. Because there are often various forms under which a particular subject might be listed, the dictionary catalog contains frequent *see* references.

For example:

Chemical geology, *see* Geochemistry

Physics, Biological, *see* Biological physics

SUBJECT HEADING CATALOG CARDS

Once you have noted enough leads to begin, go to the card catalog's subject heading cards and start gathering information. You may find it useful at this point to begin using index cards for notes; generally it is a good idea to begin each new listing on a separate card. If your notes from given works are likely to be extensive, then you will use index cards only to record bibliographic details. The cards will later prove invaluable in assembling an index for your final product, in arranging and rearranging your materials for chapter or topic subdivision of the work, and for footnoting or otherwise annotating the references you cited.

Here is the information typically to be found on an entry in the card catalog (see Figure 3):

1. *Call Number.* This group of several lines of letters and/or numbers is used by libraries to classify and properly shelve the work. Copy all of the symbols, found in the upper left corner of the card, exactly as shown, including punctuation marks.

2. *Author's name and years of birth and death.* The card will indicate the full name, and will bracket parts of the name not used in a particular publication, e.g.,

   Fenner, P[eter].

   When only the year of birth is listed the author was alive at the time of publication of the edition of the work cataloged. Missing dates signify only that they were unknown by the cataloger.

3. *Title of the work.* Subtitles will be included.

4. *Place of publication.* City of publication; further place information is omitted except to avoid ambiguity.

5. *Publisher.* Important for purchases and to determine reputation.

6. *Date of Publication.* This will help you distinguish among different editions of a work. Larger libraries have most editions of important works. Differences among editions may be critical for your work.

7. *Physical description.* The number of pages shown will be listed separately for front matter and numbered text pages. Presence of illustrations will be noted. Spine height is given in centimeters. If not a regular book, size and shape of materials are noted.

8. *Description.* One or more sentences may be used to describe

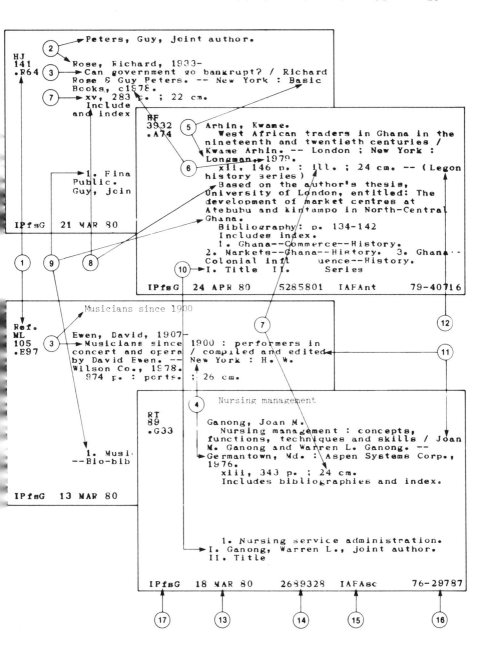

Figure 3. Labelled parts of sample library catalog cards. The circled numbers refer to numbered paragraphs in the accompanying text. At top are author and added-author cards; below are title cards.

the work or to add points of interest about it. Bibliography and index information is given when appropriate.

9. *Subject tracings.* These listings give you important clues about where else you might look for information. These lines are particularly helpful when the item you want is unavailable for your use.

10. *Added entries.* Other authors, series listings note, later editions of the same work, or similar notes or cross-references.
    I. Coauthors
    II. Series of which this work is a part
    III. Other kinds of cross-references

11. *Statement of responsibility.* A listing of all authors, editors, compilers, or the like.

12. *Series.* If the work is one of a series of publications or materials, this is noted.

Individual libraries or library systems often add several other marks to the cards. Examples of some used in one library:

13. *Library's accession date.*

14. *OCLC accession number.* Formerly representing the Ohio College Library Consortium, OCLC has become an initialism free of contextual meaning; however, the computer base is actively maintained, and standardized numbers are issued for works logged into that system.

15. *Library's OCLC access code.*

16. *Library of Congress accession number.*

17. *Internal code.*

EVALUATION OF CARD CATALOG ENTRIES

While there is no substitute for actually examining a book, the catalog card can give you clues about the potential suitability of a work.

The publication date will give you some idea about when the research for the book must have been completed, and how up-to-date the work will be. You must weigh the relative importance of historical background and the latest research findings, then guess for which purpose the book is likely to serve better.

The reputation or the authority of an author may be evident to you. This could be a result of recognizing the author's name from other works you have studied; it may be the result of association with a collaborator with whose works or reputation you are familiar; or, it may simply be due to seeing several works listed under the same author's name in the card catalog.

If the book contains a bibliography, the catalog card indicates its length in pages. Especially in the early phases of research, and in assessing the potential worthiness of a review book, this can be very important information.

The edition number suggests whether an older work is sufficiently well thought of by the buying public to be revised and reprinted. It also tells you whether or not the work is being kept up to date through revised editions.

Last, the publisher's reputation may give you a clue about the dependability of the work. The major publishers tend to put sufficient energy into a work to make it reliable. University presses generally seek carefully researched specialty works. Some smaller specialty publishers usually devote extra energy to the publication of the few works they produce. Self-published and privately published works may be carefully prepared and printed. However, because self-published works are subjected to little scrutiny beyond that of their authors, some are poorly done.

CLASSIFICATION SYSTEMS

Most institutional libraries use one of two major systems of classification for all holdings:

Dewey Decimal System
Library of Congress Classification System

Under the Dewey Decimal System, books and other materials are distributed by classification according to these general categories:

000–099	General Works
100–199	Philosophy & Psychology
200–299	Religion
300–399	Social Science
400–499	Languages
500–599	Pure Science
600–699	Applied Science & Technology
700–799	Fine Arts
800–899	Literature
900–999	History, Biography, Geography

Each of these ten major categories is further subdivided, first by most important divisions, then by successively smaller subdivisions. As many decimal places as might be needed can be used to further subdivide the category into niches as detailed as desired.

In both systems, additional lines of letters or numbers are used to identify authors, editions, and the like. These numbers and the finer subdivisions of each system's main entry frequently differ from one library to another. In the case of authorship, this has to do with the designators previously used for an author in a library. In the case of the main category's subdivision, it has more to do with cataloging conventions used by a library. For example, will a library adopt the number assigned by the Library of Congress for its holdings (many libraries now do this, because catalog cards may be obtained, pre-printed, with that information already provided), or are there reasons (usually pertaining to specialized holdings) why a library might want to modify the suggested Library of Congress number?

In any event, the Library of Congress publishes *The Library of Congress classification schedules*, annually indexed and amended, to include all numbers it has assigned. These volumes are of immense importance to all catalogers.

In the Library of Congress System, call numbers begin with an initial capital letter that divides knowledge into broad areas. A second letter, followed by numbers, further subdivides the subject of the book. The call numbers assigned partly reflect the acquisition schedule as much as they do a natural classification system. Books typically have the call numbers marked on their spines or front covers; other materials show the number in obvious locations. Figure 4 shows call numbers taken from books labelled with *Library of Congress* system numbers.

All works within a collection are shelved alphanumerically, letter-by-letter and line-by-line, with full observance of decimal placement.

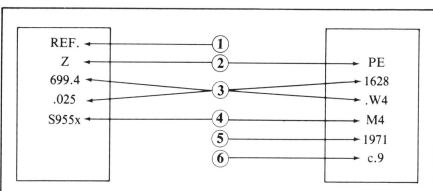

Figure 4. Call numbers from the spines of G. & C. Merriam Co.'s Webster's Seventh New Collegiate Dictionary *(left), and SDC* Search Service's ORBIT Quick Reference Guide *(right). Legend:*

① *Shelved in special collection (Reference)*
② *LC subject classification letter(s)*
③ *LC classification number (may include letters)*
④ *Library's author & title code*
⑤ *Edition*
⑥ *Copy number for this library*

Blank spaces are not observed. Thus, e.g., here are some call numbers arranged in proper shelf sequence:

QA	QA	QA	QA	QA	QB	QB	QC	R	S
76	76	76	76	76	300	301	89	210	560
.A8	.A82	.C6	.D32	.D4	...	...	...	...	...

If your library has open stacks (i.e., stacks accessible to you), make it a habit always to look at other works with the same or nearly the same classification symbols as the one you seek. This can help you to find additional useful information on your topic.

SELF-TEST

After having reviewed the filing conventions used in your library, take this self-test. You should be able to get at least 5 of the 6 sets of questions completely correct. Once you have attained that level of competence, go on to Chapter 2.

First, here is the test. In the blank spaces provided, list the sequence (1 = first, 3 or 4 = last) in which the filing cards should be alphabetized. Be aware that from one library system to another the answers could differ.

1. _____ McCalister, Wayd Hampton
   _____ The macrophage
   _____ MacDonald, Doughald
   _____ MacDonald, Hamish

2. _____ Dont, Jacob
   _____ Donovan, Timothy Paul
   _____ Don't be afraid

3. _____ The ABC World Airways Guide
   _____ AAAS Conference on Science Teaching
   _____ And they shall walk
   _____ Aa, Pieter van der

4. _____ One hundred best books
   _____ 125 simple home repairs
   _____ 110 tested plans
   _____ One hundred and five sonnets

5. _____ Time remembered
   _____ Time, Mark
   _____ Time, a monthly magazine: v.1–24: April 1879–91. London
   _____ The Times (London)

6. _____ LIFE-BOATS (subject)
   _____ LIFE (BIOLOGY) (subject)
   _____ LIFE-ORIGIN (subject)
   _____ LIFE (Chicago) (subject)

Using Basic Library Procedures   2

INTRODUCTION

Each library is unique. Holdings differ. Layouts differ. Procedures are different. **This chapter will help you review or learn procedures to locate your library's holdings.**

Do you believe that you understand *your* library's layout and procedures? Try the self-test at the end of this chapter. If you cannot pass the test with at least twenty-seven correct answers (90%) accuracy, then read on. Also, note that many libraries and learning resources centers offer self-guided tours, audiotaped or videotaped orientations, and often elaborately printed guides and floorplans. Do take the tour and study the plan of your library—if they are available.

The following pages describe some aspects of the library of a typical, modern, medium-sized state university. Institutional philosophy—whether of a municipal library system, a private research organization, or a state institution—as much as size, will affect the level of detail and the intra-institutional spread of library holdings. Consider how your library addresses the variables mentioned here.

HOLDINGS

How extensive are the holdings in your library? Our typical library has about 200,000 books, 3000 journal subscriptions, many audiotapes, videotapes, phonodiscs, motion picture films and loop films, microform collections, slides, kits, biologic and geologic display and study materials, and other realia. Cooperative arrangements with nearby libraries and library systems provide rapid access to nearly *fifty times* as many items.

SYSTEM OF CLASSIFICATION

The Library of Congress system of classification has evolved from many decades of work at the Library of Congress in Washington, D.C. While this system has its roots in other classification schemes, it is designed specifically for the Library of Congress and for no other. However, other libraries, and particularly many with large collections, have found the system usable and have adopted or adapted it for their own use. This system divides all knowledge into main subject groups; letters of the alphabet are used as the primary dividers. It provides a viable and flexible scheme with gaps for growth. For example, the letters I, O, W, X, and Y have not yet been used as main subject divisions. Each of the main groups, or classes, can be divided into additional and narrower subject groups by adding a second letter; further subdivision is accomplished by adding from 1 to 4 digits. In order to make the classification numbers unique for each piece of material, Library of Congress catalogers add a sequence of alphabetic and numeric characters to denote particular authors. A unique call number for each title in the collection is extremely important for shelving and accountability purposes.

Our library uses the *LC* system. Does yours?

TYPES OF ACCESS FILES IN THE LIBRARY

Card Catalog

This is usually in front of the Circulation Desk, and is almost certainly familiar enough to you not to need any explanation. Some of the other files listed below may be less familiar.

Pamphlet File

This is also known as the vertical file. It includes ephemeral materials such as articles and pamphlets. These materials, which are frequently weeded, represent the most recent or the only information available on a particular subject. They are usually articles of a few pages and are seldom listed in standard bibliographies or indexes. You won't find the file's contents listed in the card catalog. Instead, an alphabetical index of subject headings included in the file is located with the file. Cross-references are given.

Where is your library's vertical file?

Periodicals Holdings List

Periodicals and other journals are housed in a separate collection in most libraries. Sometimes they are arranged by classification number (subject). Often, however, they are arranged alphabetically by title, with microfilm, bound volumes, and current issues standing together. Newspapers are kept only a few months, with the backfiles on microfilm. The *Periodical Holdings List* indicates the dates included for all periodical holdings.

Indexes and Abstracts

Indexes are one of several types of systematic guides available for given bodies of literature, especially journals and books. They usually provide complete bibliographic information, which is arranged in some readily accessible manner, such as in alphabetical or chronological order, by author, by subject, or according to some other numerical coding scheme. Frequently a summary or abstract is included with the bibliographic information.

In an abstract journal, abstracts are accompanied by bibliographic information. Contents are arranged as in an index.

In many libraries, the indexes and abstracts are arranged alphabetically by title and are shelved together near the periodicals and journals to which they provide access. *A Subject Guide to Indexes and Abstracts* provides increased accessibility.

Reference Material

Encyclopedias, dictionaries, directories, indexes and abstracts, atlases, gazetteers, yearbooks, bibliographies, and other similar works are comprehensive compilations, condensed and arranged in some logical sequence in order to make their information readily accessible to the user.

Before using a reference book of this type, it is wise to examine the title page for date of publication and other bibliographic information and to read the preface or introduction to determine its intended purpose and how best to use it. Rarely can these materials be used outside the library.

Some reference holdings may be interfiled in the general collection; these can be checked out.

SPECIAL CATEGORY MATERIALS

Government Publications

Government publications are books, periodicals, and other documents distributed in quantity at the initiative and under the seal of an agency of government—e.g., by countries, states, counties, districts, provinces, and municipalities. They provide primary information for the study of governmental structures, function, and influence, and cover a broad spectrum of subjects.

State depository libraries receive a paper or microfiche copy of all state government publications that the State Library receives from state agencies in sufficient quantity to disseminate throughout the depository library system. In our system, the main card catalog is the chief means for locating state documents, each one of which is entered under its authors and/or issuing agency, title, and subjects. A symbol—e.g., DOCS—usually appears on each catalog card above the classification number, identifying it as an item shelved separately in the *Documents Collection.*

Selective United States federal depository libraries receive some series of the federal documents made available to them. These documents are arranged by the U.S. Superintendent of Documents' classification scheme and are usually separately housed. The number appearing on each federal document is called a SuDocs classification number, and is determined by reference to the *Monthly Catalog, United States Government Publications*. The *Monthly Catalog* is arranged by agencies and indexed by authors, titles, and subjects. The *Documents Shelflist*, usually located nearby, will tell you whether or not your library has received specific documents; the *Shelflist* is arranged in SuDocs classification order. Selected federal documents are fully cataloged in the main card catalog and are shelved under the SuDocs number with all the other uncataloged federal documents. DOCS notation on these catalog cards may indicate shelving in a separate *Documents Collection*.

Governmental periodicals are usually intershelved alphabetically with other items in the *Periodicals Collection*. Indexes and abstracts of government publications are intershelved alphabetically in the Index Area of the library, except for the *Monthly Catalog* and *Monthly Checklist of State Publications*, which may be shelved on the Documents index tables. Periodicals, indexes, and abstracts published by the state or federal government are listed in the *Periodicals Holdings List*.

Special indexes, such as *Document Catalog, Monthly Checklist*, and the *American Statistics Index*, can also be used to find government publications. They are usually shelved in the Index Area or the *Reference Collection* and are listed in the main card catalog with appropriate location symbols.

Media

Nonprint materials, films, slides, records, cassettes, games, models, videotapes, motion picture loops, transparencies, and realia are usually listed in the card catalog by title, author, and subject in the same way print materials are listed. Your library may also maintain a separate listing for those materials. Art slides, videotapes, 16mm films, and phonodiscs (records) may be housed in a separate media area. All other media are sometimes intershelved in the general collection.

Microforms

Advantages of microforms include their efficient storage, ready availability, low cost, and the ease with which page copies may be obtained from them. They also have disadvantages: because reading devices must be used, most users must read in the library; use of such devices may be tiring for some users; and, some users object to any book substitute.

The most common microform is *microfilm*. It stores documents at reduction ratios from 15:1 to 20:1 on reels of 35mm film. The *micro-card*, typically an opaque card measuring 4 by 6 inches, can store 60 to 80 pages of documents, magazines, or newspapers. *Microfiches* are cards with regular microfilm mounted in apertures; they use about the same reduction ratios as microcards. *Minicards* the size of postage stamps contain images reduced about 60:1, and *ultrafiches* use reduction ratios of 200:1 or even 400:1. The latter are usually prepared for specific commercial applications, for use with customized readers.

Guide to Microforms in Print and *Subject Guide to Microforms in Print*, both published annually by Microcard Editions, Inc., alphabetically list all microforms available for general purchase in the United States. Books are listed by authors, periodicals and newspapers by title, and archival materials by publisher. Dissertations are not listed.

Microform collections may include back issues of periodicals, microfiches of the Educational Research Information Center (ERIC) document file, *Envirofiche*, National Technical Information Service (NTIS) documents, *Disclosure* (corporate reports to the Securities and Exchange Commission), the Human Relations Area File (HRAF), thousands of college catalogs, and the like.

Materials Center and Other Special Collections

Textbooks, curriculum materials, juvenile fiction and non-fiction, and media of use to the elementary or secondary school teacher may be housed separately in a *Materials Center*. Sample curriculum guides would be used in preparing classes, sample textbooks give an overview of materials available, and special juvenile literature might include Newberry and Caldecott medal winners, literature, and selections of material from various publishers. Rare book collections, major donated collections, research collections, and the like, may also be housed separately. Typically their contents are listed separately and in the main card catalog.

Oversize Materials

Any item that will not fit on regular shelves is shelved in the Oversize Area. In its place in the regular stacks, a wooden "dummy" book usually direct patrons to the Oversize Area.

OTHER NOTES

Learn the rules used by your library about reserve materials, charging materials out, fines, patrons reshelving books, identification required to use the facilities, hours of the library, and the detection system. Knowing these in advance can save you much inconvenience.

SELF-TEST

After studying this chapter and a guide to your particular library or learning resources center, you should be able to score at least 27 correct answers for these 30 questions.

For the following questions, identify the best answer(s) among choices given: write in a better answer if none of those given fits. Give answers that apply to *your* library or resources center.

1. Which card in the card catalog contains the most extensive information about a book?
    a. the author card
    b. the title card
    c. they all contain the same information
    d. the subject heading card
    e. other: _____

2. Where is the information about your state's documents to be found?
    a. in the document catalog
    b. in the author-title catalog
    c. in both catalogs
    d. in another catalog, namely: _____
    e. there are no government documents in the holdings

3. If there are federal documents, where are they housed?
    a. separate from the general collection
    b. interfiled with the general collection
    c. in building _____
       —or, if there are no government documents,
    d. where is the nearest repository for government documents? _____

4. Of the following items, which would appear first in the author-title file of the card catalog?
    a. The Trials of John Muir
    b. 20th Century Typography
    c. Thomas, David
    d. Tsetse Flies and Trypanosomes

5. Of the following items, which would appear last in the author-title file in the card catalog?
    a. The Trials of John Muir
    b. 20th Century Typography

   c. Thomas, David

   d. Tsetse Flies and Trypanosomes

6. Which of these materials are not to be found in the audio-visual catalog or media list?

   a. 35mm slides

   b. 16mm films

   c. 8mm films

   d. phonodiscs

   e. videotapes

   f. kits

   g. games

   h. all of the above, because we have no such catalog

7. All audio-visual materials are listed in:

   a. the audio-visual catalog(s)

   b. the main catalog

   c. both of the above

   d. other: _____

   e. none of the above, because our library hasn't such materials

8. The quickest way to locate the book *Science & Technology*, by Grogan, would be to:

   a. search the *Applied Science and Technology Index*

   b. go directly into the stacks, looking under *Ap*

   c. search the card catalog under the author's name

   d. see the reference librarian

   e. other: _____

9. If you have difficulty with audio-visual materials or equipment, which person would be most likely to help you?

   a. reference librarian

   b. buildings and grounds electrician

   c. media desk staff

   d. liaison librarian

   e. other: _____

10. Theoretically, the classification scheme in the library uses:

   a. A to Z

   b. .1 to 999.99

   c. A1 to Z999

   d. 000 to 999

11. Which of the following materials are not found in the library?
    a. state documents
    b. geological maps of the continental USA
    c. atlas describing lunar topography
    d. different types of soil samples
    e. all are found in my library
12. Audiotapes are intermingled with the general collection.
    a. true
    b. false, they are housed: _____
    c. false, the library hasn't any audiotapes
13. Videocassettes are intermingled with the general collection.
    a. true
    b. false, they are housed: _____
    c. false, there are none in the library
14. After locating a book on the shelf and examining it for a while, you decide you will not charge it out. You should:
    a. put it back near the spot where you found it
    b. reshelve it in the exact spot where you found it
    c. put it on top of the card catalog
    d. give it to a staff person behind the circulation desk
    e. put it on any carrel shelf
    f. other: _____
15. The length of time reserve materials may be checked out is:
    a. two weeks
    b. two hours or three days
    c. three days
    d. determined by librarians who put the works on reserve
    e. other: _____
16. Phonograph records are housed separately from the general collection.
    a. true
    b. false, because they are interfiled
    c. false, because there are no phonograph records in the collection
    d. false, because there is no general collection
17. To find out whether your library subscribes to *Geotimes* and ascertain the inclusive dates, you should:
    a. locate the title in the card catalog

b. refer to the *Periodical Holdings* catalog

c. check the *Readers Guide to Periodical Literature*

d. ask the reference librarian

e. look under *Ge* in the periodical stacks

f. other: _____

18. Government documents are excellent sources of environmental information. They may be found by:

a. checking the main card catalog under the issuing agency

b. can't be found here; I must go to: _____

c. finding the item desired in the *Monthly Catalog* with its GPO classification and then looking for it by its GPO classification number in the stacks

d. searching the documents catalog under the issuing agency or the title

e. searching the document stacks, which are arranged alphabetically by issuing agency

19. If your library's collections include the fiche collection of ERIC, how can you get a copy of a document?

a. borrow it and have it copied by machine at your own expense

b. have the Circulation Desk make a copy at no charge

c. you can't, but are allowed to review it on a fiche reader

d. other: _____

20. ERIC documents on fiches are filed:

a. alphabetically by author

b. sequentially by the code number, such as ED003951

c. alphabetically by issuing agency

d. alphabetically by title

21. The chief means of determining the SuDocs number for federal documents is through:

a. the main card catalog

b. the *Documents Holdings Shelflist*

c. a *KWIC Index*

d. the *Monthly Catalog of U.S. Government Publications*

22. How are specialized periodicals housed?

a. with back issues separate from current issues

b. with back issues filed together with current issues

c. without back issues

23. Reference books are:
    a. interfiled with the general collection
    b. interfiled with Documents
    c. filed separately in the Reference area
    d. other: _____
24. Reference books may be checked out:
    a. never
    b. overnight & Sunday
    c. for one week
    d. only with a deposit
    e. other: _____
25. What is the charge-out period for books under general circulation?
    a. 7 days
    b. 14 days
    c. 4 weeks
    d. 1 month
    e. other: _____
26. Works in the library are arranged by:
    a. the Dewey Decimal Classification
    b. the Universal Decimal Classification
    c. Ranganathan's Colon Classification
    d. the Library of Congress Classification
    e. other: _____
27. Where are the microfiches kept?
    a. in the Documents collection
    b. in fiche cabinets, located: _____
    c. interfiled in the general collection
    d. with the periodicals
    e. near the Media Desk
    f. other: _____
28. To be sure of using the correct terminology in searching for a particular subject in the card catalog, it is best to check:
    a. *The Library of Congress Subject Headings*
    b. *Webster's Unabridged Dictionary*
    c. *Oxford English Dictionary*
    d. *EJC (Engineering Joint Commission) Thesaurus*
    e. *Sears Subject Headings*

29. Oversize materials that will not fit on regular shelves are accommodated by:

   a. shelving them behind the Circulation Desk

   b. shelving them in a separate section located: _____

   c. shelving them in the Reference section

   d. interfiling with other materials, and laying them flat on the shelves

30. How are the cards arranged in the main card catalog?

   a. word-by-word, except when a chronological or numerical arrangement is used for clarity

   b. letter-by-letter

   c. dictionary arrangement

   d. other: _____

Identifying Literature Classes

INTRODUCTION

There are important differences among the types of literature sources from which you can collect scientific data. The type of source you use may influence both your interpretation of data and your conclusions. **This chapter will help you learn to discriminate the characteristics of pre-primary, primary, secondary, and tertiary sources of scientific literature.**

The lines between the pre-primary, primary, secondary, and tertiary classes of scientific and technical literature are often obscure. A given publication may include contributions that belong to more than one class. Our purpose here is to attune you to variations in standards of accuracy, currency, completeness, and validity among the different classes. Information-transfer experts may argue about where to draw the lines between classes or about the proper class of a particular writing, but they do not argue about the marked differences among the classes.

For example, D. H. Michael Bowen[1] defined a primary publication as one "that publishes information written by the generator of the information, or written by him and rewritten by someone else . . ." He noted five types: scientific journals, technical journals, trade press books, general magazines and non scientific journals. He concluded that "The most reliable information . . . is to be found in publications that are the most expensive, the least available, and the most difficult to read and understand. . . . [P]ublications that are inexpensive, easy to read, and easily available tend to sacrifice accuracy and scientific objectivity." Information at both ends of the spectrum is necessary. You should be aware of what kind you use.

PRE-PRIMARY LITERATURE

Bowen's paper is an example of *pre-primary* literature—literature that "is largely accessible to an in-group of specialists, frequently called the invisible college, is invariably free and most useful to them, and is impossibly difficult for others to get hold of. Much pre-primary information is public information that is never formally published; it includes company technical reports, research progress reports, laboratory memorandums, and early drafts of papers that will be published—often after a delay of years."[2]

PRIMARY LITERATURE

Fenner and Lloyd defined *primary* publications as those "in which
appear the first formal results of investigations, general data, discussions and syntheses of particular data, and miscellaneous information such as that to be found in annals, festschrifts, transactions, and
proceedings. Most scientific journals appear in this group, and the
greatness of a library is determined largely by the depth and breadth
of its holdings in this category.

Pre-primary and primary literature is produced nearly exclusively by experts for experts.[3] One important distinction between
these categories concerns the reviewing process. Primary literature
appearing in scientific and technical journals has almost invariably
undergone critical peer review. Other scientists, specialists in the
same or closely related scientific or technical field, have read the
contribution to help ensure scientific accuracy and objectivity.
Reviewers are often in a position to recommend changes, expose
additional literature, and make known more recent advances to an
author. This process tends to upgrade the literature; and, it is time-
consuming. It also results in a second important distinction between
these two literature types: pre-primary literature is often rushed to
print—sometimes prematurely—as a result of program pressures for
meetings, and the like. The invisible college, those researchers at the
forefront of knowledge in a given field, benefit most from pre-primary
literature, and are understanding of errors that appear there. It is not
uncommon for senior researchers to make major revisions in their
public presentations at professional meetings in response to contributions (oral or written) of a colleague received only minutes or hours
earlier.

As a side note, we find it interesting that in 1977 Bonn cited
reliable earlier estimates that the world total of scientific and technical periodicals was about 35,000 titles, the average number of articles
published by each being about 65 per year in 1966. Articles published, he estimated, would double in 10–15 years; this contention is
supported by Ziman.[4] Bonn wrote that at least 100 countries add to
the serial literature of science and technology, publishing in any of
about 40 different languages, irrespective of country of origin. Excepting the Chinese literature of science, to which no reference was
made, 50% of the materials counted by Bonn appeared in English,
14% in Russian, 10% in German, 9% in French, and 4% in Japanese.
Fenner and Lloyd estimated 15,000 serial titles for the geological
literature—an estimate based on a pre-primary source, a report of a
work then in progress and already listing more than 10,000 titles.
Those serials were estimated to present 40,000 formal geological

papers annually. Including other literature types (pre-primary, secondary, and tertiary), 80,000 to 100,000 published and public papers dealing with some aspect of geology were expected in 1970—a figure then projected to double by 1980. They estimated 100,000 as the total serial titles for all science and technology (all classes), including about 1850 [abstracts journals,] in 1970. The scope of the literature access problem is exemplified, using the 1965 data cited by Fenner and Lloyd, by the chemistry literature. *Chemical Abstracts* then abstracted about 200,000 titles (95−97% of all published chemistry papers) from about 10,000 journals, of which some 1000 serials accounted for 75% of the abstracts, 250 for 50%, and 100 for 33%. These data may help to explain the importance of the secondary literature—especially to emerging libraries.

SECONDARY LITERATURE

Secondary publications are based on information derived from primary sources. They include indexes, abstracting journals, and review journals. For the nonspecialist scientific reader they are perhaps the best source for general information. Their quality varies from top-drawer to barely worthy of the recycling bin.

The line separating secondary and tertiary sources may be vague, especially among certain specialized handbooks and encyclopedias.

By means of extensive indexing, annotated bibliographies, selective state-of-the-art summaries, and collections of comprehensive and definitive reviews, the secondary literature tends to be the most ready source of current scientific and technical information. However, workers at the frontiers of science use this literature only for work outside their areas of expertise; the 1- or 2-year lag time to publication of secondary material is usually intolerable to members of the invisible college.

Encyclopedias and handbooks or manuals may be secondary or tertiary literature, depending upon their specificity.

TERTIARY LITERATURE

Tertiary publications include texts and reference books, most handbooks, and the like. As Bonn (1977, p. 615) puts it, they are often *about* rather than *of* science. They are invariably several years out of date but are necessary compendiums of information. They are rational syntheses of all the other categories. Literature guides (as opposed, for example, to indexing journals) and directories belong to the tertiary literature.

Depending on the specificity or generality of their contents, certain reference works, such as encyclopedias, dictionaries, handbooks, and critical tables, may be considered as either secondary or tertiary works. Certain advanced textbooks, on the other hand, may resemble monographs and thus be akin to secondary (and sometimes, though rarely, primary) literature—the rigor of treatment, scope of coverage, and depth of systematic development determine their classification. Symposium publications may fall into any category, from pre-primary to tertiary.

Develop your skill in recognizing the type of source your information comes from, so that you can use it with appropriate skepticism or assurance.

STUDY QUESTIONS

If you are still uncertain of the distinctions among the classes of literature discussed in the foregoing pages, read further in the cited works or seek out other references to give you additional insight. Remember as you read, that the point is not so much to be able to classify everything you read as it is to understand that the currency and reliability of what you read in the various classes of literature may vary.

For the following questions, identify the best answer(s) among the choices given. Remember that some classifications are matters of interpretation. You should, nonetheless, be able to score at least 18 correct answers on the 20 questions given. For questions 4–18, explain any assumptions you make.

1. Which class of literature has the lowest ease of access?
   a. pre-primary
   b. primary
   c. secondary
   d. tertiary
2. Which class of literature is most reliable and accurate?
   a. pre-primary
   b. primary
   c. secondary
   d. tertiary
3. Which class of literature is the least up-to-date?
   a. pre-primary
   b. primary
   c. secondary
   d. tertiary

Categorize each of the following titles or publications as to class. Note the inconsistent citation system, reflective of the literature.

4. Condensed chemical dictionary

5. Dictionary of medical specialists

6. SDC technical memorandum 34-C-219: Study of cost-effectiveness of computer-controlled retrieval system in Santa Monica Public Library

7. Industrial Research Laboratories of the U.S.

8. Anatomy of the human body

9. Casagrande, Daniel J., 1970, Geochemistry of Aminoacids in selected Florida peats, Thesis, Pennsylvania State University.

10. Bibliography of American Natural History

11. Fosdick, F., "Pollution of Thorn Creek, 1970–73."

12. DATRIX (direct access to reference of information; a Xerox service). Ann Arbor, Michigan, University Microfilms. Doctoral dissertations since 1938 in American universities.

13. Style guide for chemists

14. "Handbook of geochemistry"

15. *Guide to the geologic literature*

16. Fon, Liang T., et al. "Solid Waste—plastics composites; physical properties and feasibility for production," *Environmental Science and Technology,* 6, 1085–1091, December 1972

17. Source book of biological names and terms

18. Progress report NIH grant: 01-0400-932001: Curriculum Development for Competency-based Nursing Education

19. Research Grants Index

20. Harper Encyclopaedia of Science

NOTES

1. "Scientific and technical primary publications carrying environmental information;" unpublished pre-print: Cincinnati, Ohio, National Environmental Information Symposium, September 24–27, 1972, (pp. 1–9).

2. Peter Fenner and Joel Lloyd, 1970, "Serials important to geologists," *Geotimes,* v. 15 (July/August, p. 14).

3. For an author who does not distinguish pre-primary and primary literature, see George S. Bonn, author of the 1977 article, "Literature of science and technology," appearing in the 3rd edition of the *McGraw-Hill Encyclopedia of Science and Tech-*

nology. According to Bonn (1977, pp. 611–613), the primary literature often provides the only published accounts of new research and developments in science and technology—those appearing nearly exclusively in periodicals, separate research reports, patents, dissertations, or manufacturers' technical bulletins. Availability of certain classes of research reports and data on patent literature are discussed by Bonn.

4. J. M. Ziman, 1980, in "The proliferation of scientific literature: a natural process," *Science*, *208*, pp. 369–371, claims that in recent years the growth has slowed to about 2–3% per annum—in terms of titles, not necessarily pages printed.

Planning a Literature Search　　4

INTRODUCTION

Knowing how information is organized can help you conduct a systematic search of the literature pertinent to a particular research area. **This chapter should help you be able to plan a literature search and find the best sources to answer specific information questions.**

For a scientist, a literature search is more habit than project. The researcher remains a life-long student, always preparing for work that is never finished, striving to remain current with the growth of knowledge in relevant areas. This kind of reading, or directed skimming of professional literature, is more routine than daily newspaper skimming. Realizing that some 10,000 to 20,000 articles in science and technology are published every working day of the year underscores the importance of this habit. Scientific researchers are acquainted (by title skimming, if no more) with the progress of science as reflected in the twenty to forty journals and other periodicals they regularly skim. Researchers read mainly the pre-primary and primary literatures.

One gains the research habit slowly, by making one literature search after another until it becomes a painless, enjoyable process that opens the gate to a world of knowledge.

A few words of caution: don't be fooled by skeptics who claim that literature merely confuses, that it is a waste of time, or that much can be gained by an "open mind" approach. Beveridge (1971, p. 5) answers that claim by quoting Lord Byron: "To be perfectly original one should think much and read little, and this is impossible, for one must have read before one has learnt to think." He also quotes Bacon (p. 6) in urging the novice to distinguish research results and experimenters' interpretations of them: "Read not to contradict and confute, nor to believe and take for granted ... but to weigh and consider." You should, in other words, be as careful in your reading as you are in your writing to distinguish among fact, opinion, conclusion, judgment, influence, and the like. If your literature searches relate to a research interest of yours, you might well agree with Wilson (1952, p. 10): "Six hours in the library may save six months in the laboratory."

THE SEARCH—IN PRINCIPLE

Often the most expeditious route to follow in researching a subject is to go from general information to specific. Broadly stated, this may mean working from tertiary or secondary towards primary or, if available, pre-primary information sources. Working toward the specific, you will become more familiar with the names of workers in the area and of research centers where relevant work is carried out. This may open the door to personal inquiry and later, perhaps, admission to the invisible college. It also provides the investigator with the most convenient reference source, the reprint.

Many different schemes exist for the collection of notes and personal indexes. The single-purpose search for data that are primarily bibliographic, and that must only be retrieved once, will usually best make use of ordinary index cards—cards that can then be arranged and rearranged prior to some final report preparation. Using one card for a single citation, note, source or author, chronological event in a sequence, or solitary category among many allows these variables to be ordered, reordered, coded, and cross-indexed; the cards can even be edge-marked for ease of specific data access. Hand-punched cards used with needle-sorting devices, and computer-managed storage/retrieval systems are worth considering only when the data base is very large, complex, or to be accessed by many researchers—such as in a research group.

THE SEARCH—IN PRACTICE

The choice of a research topic and the library search for information about it are interrelated. As information is uncovered, the research topic may be redefined. New references must then be read and evaluated for relevance. You may find so much material on a topic that you don't know where to begin reading. On the other hand, the unavailability of one article may discourage you from looking elsewhere for the same information. If you find no starting point, reëxamine your topic.

One place to begin your search is the reference collection. Move from general to more specific reference works. Prepare a list of subject headings that appear to be relevant; list terms that help delimit your topic research. Review your progress at frequent intervals. Information you find early on may cause you to change directions, suggesting sometimes a narrowing, sometimes a broadening of the subject headings to be searched. As you find titles that promise to be helpful, make spot evaluations to help screen them: consider the publication dates of books and articles, be aware of the authorship, evaluate the quality of the journal or the publisher, and be cognizant of probable overlap among works found previously and subsequent titles.

Another approach is to search for, or ask your reference librarian to help you locate, an authoritative summary of the general area in which you are interested. There you will find definitions of relevant technical terms, you will get a quick overview of the topic, and very likely you will find a reasonably current bibliography citing good sources of additional information.

Your procedure will have to be tailored to your needs and topic. Below is a procedural checklist that includes types of information sources you might consult. The list is suggestive rather than exhaustive, and several entries are elaborated upon in ensuing sections of this chapter. Note that detailed information source lists comprise the bulk of Chapter 5.

Do this:

- define your search problem
- consider getting a computer printout of applicable subject entries
- locate and examine useful reference works (consider such works as: dictionaries, glossaries, encyclopedias and yearbooks, histories, biographies, directories, handbooks, field guides, manuals, tables, atlases and gazetteers, guides to the literature, bibliographies, collection catalogs, union lists of periodicals, reviews and subject-matter journals, translations, indexing and abstracting serials, and other special reference works, and government documents)
- query the feasibility of engaging in a complete computerized search at this point
- systematize useful references found (index cards?)
- if special terminology remains unclear, read a descriptive review article or general reference work about the topic
- list key words and phrases, then review subjects searched to this point
- enlarge or narrow the search's scope as required; study indexing and abstracting serials, other special reference works, then *Current Contents* to help redefine scope
- study the latest detailed review article about your topic, and begin scanning recent specialty journal articles; make a note of citations that can lead you further
- review the data you've assembled; fill in the gaps; set citation standards, or write to meet those set for you

- think through, then outline, your report, writing it with continual reference to your data sources
- finally, assemble and sequence your references, and type all the work

Always discuss with colleagues, professors, or librarians, any problems that you encounter regarding library materials or the searching process. A misshelved reference can stop you cold—especially if you haven't yet had much research practice. Professional encouragement at such a point can help.

SEARCH BOUNDARIES

Do not begin a search until you have a complete and accurate (and where appropriate: approved) statement of the search problem. Analyze it. Know its purpose. Bound the subject area and set limits on the time period to be covered (these bounds may change as the search progresses). Know your expectations for the completed product. If other people are involved in problem definition, the search itself, or product evaluation, be sure you all agree about scope, format, procedures, deadlines, responsibility, and other expectations.

Adjust the depth of treatment, scope of literature searched, class of sources examined, and number of references researched to the nature of your task. For example a five-minute radio or television interview and a thesis defense require entirely different kinds of preparation.[2]

Once you have sufficient familiarity with the special language of your subject to list keywords and phrases, prepare yourself for a search of the library's main card catalog by consulting *Library of Congress Subject Headings*.

COMPUTERIZED LISTINGS AND SEARCHES[3]

Computers can aid a literature search in several rather different ways. All take advantage of the computer's ability to sort quickly through its large store of memorized data and respond to particular questions about those data.

One computer-generated list, for example, *Science Citation Index*, cumulatively gives publication details for particular authors and their specific works. Though sometimes misleading, the length of such listings, as well as the nature of journals in which cited works appear, suggest the importance of the original writings.

Various commercial information services are available. See the section below (p. 54) and consult your reference librarian.

REFERENCE READING

Reference works are assembled for purposes other than continuous reading. Unlike primary reference sources, there is no abstract to cull out the essence of an article. When working with various reference works, you will quickly learn the different styles they represent, and find it useful to recognize different approaches, premises, standards, levels of detail, cross-referencing, authorship attribution, and the like.

Below is a discussion of some of the resources and types of references that you will use for various information searches. The next chapter lists many specific sources for each category of reference work.

DICTIONARIES, GLOSSARIES, ENCYCLOPEDIAS, AND YEARBOOKS

Subject dictionaries and specialized glossaries supply specific technical definitions and shadings of meanings, including those for many scientific terms not listed in general dictionaries. Polyglot editions list the terms or their definitions in several languages. Many of these works contain encyclopedic information, illustrations, and bibliographic references. In the card catalog they are found under the subject heading, for example:

Biology—Dictionaries

Technology—Dictionaries

Definitions of a given term may differ among dictionaries.[4] For several examples, compare entries under the same word in the *Dictionary of American Slang*, the *Oxford English Dictionary*, and any two or three American unabridged dictionaries.

Encyclopedias and their yearbooks (annual updatings) tend to be most useful for a broad first view of a field. While newer editions will give a more accurate picture of the state-of-the-art, they may slight historical or bibliographic information. You'll want to review older editions, too, if you need retrospective information.

Examine general encyclopedia articles and all relevant cross-referenced articles for summary information. Use dictionaries to ensure familiarity and understanding of the specialized vocabulary. Develop a list of definitions to be used as "see also" references when you later search for subject headings in the library's card catalog. Check as many synonymous subject headings as you can think of.

Entries in specialized dictionaries, glossaries, and encyclopedias often end with a reference (which may be coded) or a brief bibliography. Consider adding such items to your "to be searched" list.

In addition to good general encyclopedias, such as *Encyclopaedia Brittanica*, there are many specialized encyclopedias and cyclopedias. The *McGraw-Hill Encyclopedia of Science and Technology* is an example of an alphabetic arrangement of related subjects with: specific data, biographical sketches, useful abbreviations, symbols, tables, diagrams, tests, illustrations, and bibliographies for further study.

The World Almanac and Book of Facts may give you important starting data. For certain kinds of information this general reference may be more helpful and easier to use than certain specialized references.

HISTORIES

In addition to general encyclopedias, biographical dictionaries, guides to the literature, handbooks, and periodical indexes, for many questions, you will refer to histories. Histories of a subject give the main facts and names in its development, and often contain full bibliographies. General and subject histories of science and technology with comprehensive indexes may be used as encyclopedias of the subject.

BIOGRAPHIES

Well-known individuals can usually be found listed in general encyclopedias or in the library's card catalog. A quick way to find a few facts about an important scientist is to look at the catalog cards for his or her books in the author-title section. (Autobiographical works would be found there, too, if published as books.) Those author cards will furnish the following biographical information:

Dates of Birth and Death

These dates follow the name. If the author is dead, consult the various general encyclopedias and biographical dictionaries. However, if no death date is listed, assume he or she is alive, and look for more information in such books as the appropriate *Who's Who* and *American Men and Women of Science*.

Nationality

Check the city where the books were published. The place of publication is given on the catalog card after the title of the book, and often indicates the nationality of the author. To look up living Americans, use *Who's Who in America*. If the books were published in England, use the British biographical dictionary, *Who's Who*.

Profession

Is the person best known as a chemist, physicist, mathematician? There are special books you should try first for scientists. Often you can tell about the author's interests or profession from the titles and introductions to published books. Are they about ecology, oceanography, biochemistry? There are special biographical dictionaries for physicists, botanists, mathematicians, and for other areas of science.

For additional biographical material, consult the library's catalog under such subject headings as: Anatomists; Biography— Dictionaries; Engineers, American—Directories; Scientists, Catholic; Women as scientists. Don't forget to look under the scientist's name for books about him or her.

Science Citation Index may give you, albeit somewhat indirectly, some biographical material that you seek. It may lead you to works written by an author who does not appear in the card catalog or in the various directories and dictionaries. This would be especially applicable for a new author or one who publishes infrequently and then only in specialized journals.

Book-length biographies of scientists frequently contain a complete list of their publications. If a full-length biography is unavailable, general and subject dictionaries and other general reference books may help; biographies of scientists are sometimes included there.

Biographical dictionaries can be useful, though they may not include persons whose fame is recent. Collected biographies have been published in nearly all subject areas. Their listings may be brief or detailed, restricted to living or dead, or by country of birth. Transliterations and variations of spelling contribute to the difficulty in locating a name. The *Dictionary of Scientific Biography* is considered the best source of information about deceased scientists.

For magazine articles about a person, consult the *Applied Science and Technology Index*. Biographical articles and obituaries appearing in science periodicals may also be found in the various indexing and abstracting services, either under the individual's name or under the heading "Biographies" or "Obituaries."

For newspaper articles consult the *New York Times Index* under "Obituaries." The exact death date will establish the approximate time when stories might appear in other newspapers or periodicals.

DIRECTORIES

Information about authors who have written little or whose published works are recent may be difficult to find. Those actively engaged in science usually belong to one or more of the national professional societies, and might be identified through one of the society membership directories. Individual membership lists published by the societies or associations usually include the person's name, address, and affiliation, and sometimes their publications and a brief personal history.

Information about the history, organization, officers, publications, and addresses of the various learned societies can sometimes also be found in directories. Much directory information is based on data gathered a year or two prior to publication; these data often change quickly, so use them cautiously.

Directories are available of libraries of specific countries and of libraries that house special collections or are strong in particular subjects. In some directories library holdings are described in detail, in others mere listings of outstanding collections are given.

HANDBOOKS AND MANUALS

Usually written about one subject, handbooks supply charts, formulas, tables, statistical data, and historical background. They are revised frequently, sometimes yearly, to include new developments and practices. Handbooks are comprehensive in scope and condensed in treatment. They are arranged systematically to facilitate quick information retrieval by means of the table of contents. Many contain detailed alphabetical indexes, bibliographies, and references to additional information.

ATLASES

A geographical atlas is a bound collection of maps, usually arranged alphabetically by region, containing also facts and figures about places. It may be a general or special work, global or regional in scope. It may contain many kinds of maps, including topographical, climatic, geologic, economic, and political.

Indexes to atlases usually give coordinates for locating geographical features. The index may also include a gazetteer, a listing of geographical names plus descriptions. The gazetteer, or dictionary of places, is helpful if your library search requires current information about a county, state, province, or nation (e.g., present population, industries, and political affiliations). Consult the most recent editions for current information.

Special atlases are useful when photos and illustrations are needed for graphic representation of a subject, such as anatomy, astronomy, or plant pathology.

GUIDES TO THE LITERATURE

Guides to the literature of a subject identify relevant specialized dictionaries, encyclopedias, manuals, handbooks; they may identify related topics. Examples include *A Bibliography of Earth Science Bibliographies* and *Guide to Basic Information Sources in Chemistry*.

BIBLIOGRAPHIES

A bibliography may be a listing of references cited or sources used by an author in preparing a written work, in supporting findings contained in a paper, or to recommend further action on the subject of the paper or related matters. More to the point here, it may be a book or separate publication that lists sources of information on a given subject, author, field of knowledge, publisher, and so on.

Because of time consumed in manuscript completion and time elapsed in the publishing process, virtually any comprehensive published bibliography of your subject will be at least a year out of date. Update it yourself by using your library's catalog and current periodical indexes. Most professional society journals give date of receipt for manuscripts published. This will help you understand the time lag.

Bibliographies may be helpful to you in suggesting the names of the leaders in the field and the most fruitful periodicals to be searched. They may list documents, pamphlets, brochures, theses, and fringe publications that may not be covered by indexing or abstracting services.

General bibliographies are helpful in a library search because they give a wide (though never complete) survey of a subject's literature. They list specific books and sometimes include annotated descriptions of the contents of works listed.

National bibliographies list books published in or about a particular country (e.g., *National Union Catalog*).

Trade bibliographies furnish the record of printing output in a country and give descriptions of books in print plus cost and purchasing information not found in less comprehensive bibliographies (e.g., *Books in Print*).

Subject bibliographies are useful for: (*a*) verification of accuracy of titles; (*b*) finding what material exists on a given topic; (*c*) an estimate of the value of a book or article, which may be given by an annotation or by reference to a critical review; (*d*) an abstract or digest of a particular book or article or note of its contents; (*e*) information on the fundamental or best books on a subject; (*f*) biographical data about an author.

CATALOGS OF LIBRARY COLLECTIONS

The most convenient source of information on books about a subject is a library's own catalog. Because few libraries can have complete subject collections, further search is necessary in other indexes to books and book collections. The catalogs of the Library of Congress are unusually comprehensive and could be considered universal bibliographies because the Library of Congress is entitled by law to receive copies of all books copyrighted in the United States. Its present collection numbers more than 75 million items, including about 19 million pamphlets and books, several million manuscripts, and millions of photographs, pieces of music, maps, and periodicals. For example, *The National Union Catalog*, which lists the major holdings of the Library of Congress and more than 700 cooperating American libraries, contains well over 14 million cards representing more than eight million titles. Complete cataloging information is included to enable the library searcher to select material for use and to copy book citations verbatim. By including monographs, new serial and periodical titles, technical reports, maps, documents, and audio-visual materials, the Library of Congress catalogs, published annually, serve as reference books for students, educators, and scientists. The Library of Congress also contains over a million book titles in Slavic, Hebraic, Japanese, and Chinese languages, making its catalogs a useful record of foreign language books. The major national card catalogs are available in book form.

The many printed catalogs of academic and special research libraries are useful for determining a book's location. They also provide bibliographical information. Book catalogs are usually assembled from the library's author, title, and subject catalog cards. Dictionary catalogs interfile entries by author, title, or subject in a single alphabetical arrangement.

Note that catalogs never include journal articles—the most valuable source of primary information. Serial holdings are cataloged, but their contents must be ascertained from their own indexes.

TRANSLATIONS

It has been estimated that at least one million scientific articles, reports, patent specifications, and books are added to the world's libraries every year, and over half of these are written in languages that more than 50% of the world's scientists cannot read. The importance of translating services in the sciences becomes evident when one considers that 90% of the medical literature is published in English, German, French, Japanese, Italian, Spanish, and Russian.

In chemistry, these languages plus Dutch are important. Furthermore, a good part of this material appears only in periodicals.

With the development of extensive translation programs, domestic and foreign, government and private, it is possible to determine the existence, availability and location of translated scientific and technical reports, periodicals and books. Information is centralized through the cooperation of the Clearinghouse for Federal Scientific and Technical Information (CFSTI) and a translation center maintained at the John Crerar Library, Chicago.

Several indexes are available to articles and other materials that have already been translated. The major current index, *Translations Register Index*, from the Special Libraries Association, is most helpful. English-language abstracting journals are also helpful in solving the language problem. Some foreign journals are published in side-by-side translations.

REVIEW JOURNALS

Current events, new developments, and trends in most fields of science and technology may be summarized in reviews. In some fields, these periodic reviews provide indispensable critical and comprehensive summaries of recent research in scientific and technological subjects. They are especially useful to scientists wishing to keep abreast of developments outside their narrow field of specialization.

Unlike the abstract of a periodical article, which usually furnishes facts contained in the article rather than an evaluation of those facts, the review covers all the significant articles reporting progress or research in a particular subject. The periodic review is more comprehensive than the regular journal article, but less exhaustive than the book that treats every aspect of a large subject. Information is presented in a form that enables the library searcher to determine quickly whether he should read further in the periodical articles listed in the bibliographies after each review article.

Specialized review journals, such as *Earth Science Reviews*, are readily identifiable by their title. Special issues or comprehensive articles that are published by regular journals are more difficult to locate. You should look for references to them in annotated bibliographies and in journal indexes.

PERIODICALS AND SERIALS

Serials are publications issued in successive parts intended to be continued indefinitely. They include periodicals, annuals (reports, yearbooks), memoirs, proceedings, and transactions of societies. A periodical usually contains articles by several named contributors; it generally has only one distinctive title, and the successive parts or numbers are intended to appear at stated or regular intervals indefinitely. Most are published two or more times each year. Some publish only brief reports of original research; others, such as academy or society transactions, specialize in exhaustive scholarly and scientific reviews of work in an active state of development. Many scientific journals are issued as proceedings or transactions of professional scientific societies or are sponsored by such groups; some issue from government bureaus; others are published as independent enterprises. The important science journals have distinctive characters and maintain definite editorial policies over long period of time. Periodicals also include newsletters, technical and trade journals, and regularly published house organs of private organizations.

Ideally, a science collection should have access to all the periodicals in which scientific papers and articles are written, plus all back volumes of such journals. The growth of science literature can be shown by comparing the 25,000 entries in the 1925–1927 edition of the *World List of Scientific Periodicals* with the 36,000 entries in the 1934 edition, and the over 50,000 entries in the 1952 edition. The number has grown steadily until there are well over 100,000 scientific and technical journals currently published. Periodicals cumulatively present a record of scientific advancement. The story is not easily read, though, because related information is scattered among numerous articles and journals.

A union list of periodicals is similar to a union book catalog. It is arranged alphabetically by title of serials, periodicals, newspapers, or microforms to be found in the libraries of a city, region, or country. The list supplies periodical title, place of publication, and where current issues and back sets of the periodicals included in the list may be found. Union lists may be general or limited to a subject. The third edition (1965) of the *Union List of Serials* published by H. W. Wilson includes only publications issued before 1950.

New Serial Titles, published by R. R. Bowker for 1950–1970, is a multi-volume work. Using the same title, the Library of Congress updated the record for 1971–1975, cross-referencing its list to the earlier work.

United Nations depository libraries are listed in the latest revision of *Consolidated Lists of Depository Libraries and Sales Agents and Offices of the United Nations and Specialized Agencies*, issued by the UN Library in the UN Documents Series.

For a list of federal depository libraries, see the most recent September issue of the *Monthly Catalog of United States Government Publications*, issued by the U.S. Superintendent of Documents. A separate supplement issued during the first half of the year lists all U.S. Government periodicals.

State documents are held by the Library of Congress and, generally, by the State Library or the issuing agency, and also the Center for Research Libraries.

As your search progresses, use any clues you can find to add new periodical titles and document numbers to your "to look up" list. Indexing and abstracting journals may well be your mainstay, at least to lead you to the appropriate primary literature. A good list of those is included in the next chapter. An abstract contains the essence of a paper's message. It should be read with great care. Typically, hundreds of readers study abstracts for each person who reads the full paper.

The journal article is usually the primary reference source. It is likely to include the most accurate and up-to-date information—including that about equipment and procedures—because it was probably written by the person conducting the research.

INDEXES AND PERIODICAL TITLES

Other lists of periodicals will be found in the various periodical indexes. For example, *Readers' Guide to Periodical Literature* would help locate sources of information in general periodicals. (It is usually less helpful to scientists than more specialized indexes and abstracting journals.) A convenient list of current periodicals for scientists is *Applied Science and Technology Index*. In it journal titles are listed in alphabetical order of their abbreviated form used in the index. In a separate listing, the full periodical title is matched with the name and address of the publisher. Figure 5 is taken from *Applied Science and Technology Index*.

In searching with indexes, start by looking up articles in the most recent periodicals available; others may be unnecessary. When you do, remember that subject headings in indexing and abstracting journals are not necessarily consistent. Consider the lag time between the appearance of the original article and that of the index (and note that most scientific journals list the date of the original receipt of articles they print—this practice, used to establish priority of ideas, patents, taxonomic nomenclature, and the like, also lets you know how great has been the additional lag time since the ideas were submitted to the periodical that finally published the article). Wherever possible, examine copies of periodicals too recent to be included in the latest available indexes.

The most recent and often most detailed information and bibliography on a subject are usually to be found in a current published

52   RESEARCH

ACM Comm—ACM Communications
ACM Trans Math Software—ACM Transactions on Mathematical Software
AIAA J—AIAA Journal
AIChE J—AIChE Journal
ASHRAE J—ASHRAE Journal
ASLE Trans—ASLE Transactions (American Society of Lubrication Engineers)
ASTM J Test & Eval—ASTM Journal of Testing & Evaluation
ASTM Stand N—ASTM Standardization News
Acoust Soc Am J—Journal of the Acoustical Society of America
Adhesives Age—Adhesives Age
Aeronaut J—Aeronautical Journal
Air Pollut Control Assn J—Journal of the Air Pollution Control Association
Aircraft Eng—Aircraft Engineering
Am Assn Pet Geologists Bull—American Association of Petroleum Geologists Bulletin
Am Cer Soc Bull—Bulletin of the American Ceramic Society
Am Cer Soc J—Journal of the American Ceramic Society
Am Chem Soc J—Journal of the American Chemical Society
Am City & County—American City and County
Am Concrete Inst J—Journal of the American Concrete Institute
Am Dyestuff Rep—American Dyestuff Reporter
Am Ind Hygiene Assn J—American Industrial Hygiene Association Journal
Am J Phys—American Journal of Physics
Am J Sci—American Journal of Science
Am Mach—American Machinist

Tunisia
Mid-cenozoic Fortuna formation, northeastern Tunisia; record of late Alpine activity on North African cratonic margin. F. B. Van Houten. bibl(p 1060-2) maps diag Am J Sci 280:1051-62 D '80

Turkey
Remnants of a pre-late Jurassic ocean in northern Turkey; fragments of Permian-Triassic Paleo-Tethys? A. M. C. Sengör and others. bibl(p504-9) maps diags Geol Soc Bull 91:599-609 O '80

United States
Analysis of drumlin form in the northeastern and north-central United States; summary. H. H. Mills. Geol Soc Bull 91:637-9 N '80

Utah
Dragonian mammals and paleocene magnetic polarity stratigraphy North Horn formation, central Utah. Y. Tomida and R. F. Butler. bibl (p809-11) il map diags Am J Sci 280:787-811 O '80
Space-time composition patterns of late cenozoic mafic volcanism, southwestern Utah and adjoining areas. M. G. Best and others. bibl(p 1049-50) maps Am J Sci 280:1035-60 D '80

Washington (state)
About forty last-glacial Lake Missoula jökulhlaups through southern Washington. R. B. Waitt, jr. bibl(p676-9) il maps diag J Geol 88:653-79 N '80

Western states
Seismotectonic regionalization of the Great Basin, and comparison of moment rates computed from holocene strain and historic seismicity; summary. R. W. Greensfelder and others. bibl maps Geol Soc Bull 91:518-23 S '80
Tectonic implications of remagnetized upper paleozoic strata of the northern Sierra Nevada. J. L. Hannah and K. L. Verosub. bibl maps diags Geology 8:520-4 N '80

Figure 5. Samples taken from the abbreviation key and main body of an issue of Applied Science and Technology Index.

periodical article. As articles from magazines and periodicals are not listed in the Main Card Catalog, search for relevant articles by looking in the annual indexes of appropriate periodicals. You can find whether or not a particular publication is indexed or abstracted, and if so where, by looking it up in *Ulrich's Periodicals Directory*.

Indexes and abstracts exist not only for periodicals, but also for publications of learned societies, documents book reviews, or composite books.

Periodicals range from general titles, such as *Scientific American* and *Science News*, to definitive or scholarly journals. As the weekly, monthly, or quarterly issues accumulate, most libraries bind the periodicals into permanent volumes and shelve them in the periodical collection. In some libraries, many back issues are available on microfilm—often shelved with the hard copies. Most libraries either post or make available bound alphabetical lists of their periodical holdings. These often note which volume numbers of each periodical are available. Such periodical holdings lists may also include a subject listing of periodicals.

In order to locate information in periodicals on a certain subject or by a particular author, it is necessary to search in one of the many periodical indexes or abstracting journals—unless a more recent work has referred you to an issue, or you have found what you seek by browsing through journals, *Science Citation Index*, or *Current Contents*—for this purpose a hit or miss technique . . . one that is effective mainly for researchers who regularly skim many journals, so know about where to look.

Like periodical indexes, abstracts and reviews provide bibliographic citations. Some abstracts report new technological information revealed in the patent literature. Abstracts and reviews are generally more finely focussed in their subject coverage than periodical indexes.

Daily newspapers print the facts about an important scientific discovery within a day of its announcement. The date of an event is the clue needed; then an index to one newspaper will function as an index to all newspapers for subjects of general interest. Three newspaper indexes that accurately cover practically all current events worthy of note, including a great many of particular interest to scientists, are: *New York Times Index* (semi-monthly, cumulated annually); *Wall Street Journal Index* (monthly, cumulated annually); and, *Chicago Tribune Index* (quarterly, cumulated annually). All of these are thoroughly cross-referenced. Since 1972 *The Newspaper Index* has covered the *Chicago Tribune*, the *Los Angeles Times*, the *New Orleans Times-Picayune*, and the *Washington Post*.

SPECIAL REFERENCE WORKS

The *Technical Book Review Index* (published by the Special Libraries Association) is representative of works offering critical opinions about scientific books.

Computer-generated, *Science Citation Index* (*SCI*) lists two kinds of citations. Its citation index includes all works cited or indexed by each paper covered in a work included in the 2400 journals presently indexed. Its source index lists all authors of all papers listed in the first index; these listings are by author and title of each work indexed in that quarter, year, or cumulation. Figure 6 explains *SCI* graphically. Its permuterm index (see Figure 7) may also be of special help as a subject index. These bibliographic tools offer unique entry into an author's published work and related work written by others.

Current Contents is an aid to browsing in the current literature. Simply by reproducing their latest contents pages, this weekly publication displays the contents usually of more than 1000 journals in each of its editions. The six interdisciplinary science editions (e.g., the Agriculture, Biology, and Environmental Sciences edition or the Physical, Chemical, and Earth Sciences edition) and the Arts and Humanities edition give an unparalleled overview of what is now being published. Once you spot an item of interest you can seek it in your library, request an interlibrary loan, or write to its author for a reprint. Each *Current Contents* also contains a directory giving a full mailing address for the senior author of every article covered by that issue (see Figure 8). Furthermore, if a paper cannot otherwise be obtained in time, either at a library or as a reprint from the author, the publishers of *Current Contents* will send you (for a small fee) a copy of the article within 48 hours. Each issue also carries a subject index (see Figure 8). The latter is prepared by listing every significant word and phrase appearing in each title listed. (Note how carefully authors must select apt titles for their publications!)

Current Contents also summarizes or comments upon selected articles from the lay and professional literature. Among other distinctive features, each issue also identifies the languages in which journal articles appear in each journal shown. It also includes information about many scientific and technical books, monographs, conference proceedings, symposia, and the like; listings include bibliographic citations, prices, and chapter headings for each work listed.

COMPUTER DATA BASES

It is certainly no accident that *Current Contents* and *Science Citation Index* have the same publisher, a fact that highlights the power of

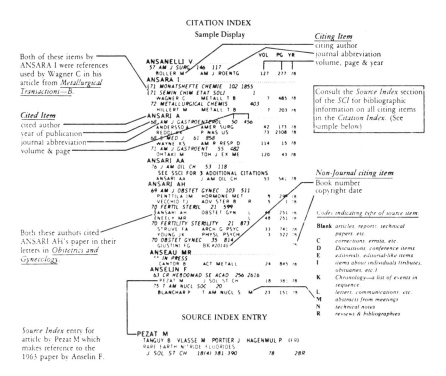

CITATION INDEX
Sample Display

Citing Item

Both of these items by ANSARA I were references used by Wagner C in his article from *Metallurgical Transactions—B.*

Cited Item
cited author
year of publication
journal abbreviation
volume & page

citing author
journal abbreviation
volume, page & year

Consult the *Source Index* section of the *SCI* for bibliographic information on all citing items in the *Citation Index*. (See sample below)

Non-Journal citing item
Book number
copyright date

Codes indicating type of source item.

Blank *articles, reports, technical papers, etc.*
C *corrections, errata, etc.*
D *Discussions, conference items*
E *editorials, editorial-like items*
I *items about individuals (tributes, obituaries, etc.)*
K *Chronology—a list of events in sequence.*
L *letters, communications, etc.*
M *abstracts from meetings*
N *technical notes*
R *reviews & bibliographies*

Both these authors cited ANSARI AH's paper in their letters in *Obstetrics and Gynecology.*

SOURCE INDEX ENTRY

Source Index entry for article by Pezat M which makes reference to the 1963 paper by Anselin F.

PATENT CITATION INDEX

When a patent is cited in a source item the arrangement of the information is altered slightly. As shown in the example below, the cited patent number is used in place of the author's last name. The Patent Section is numerically arranged. Additional information is displayed in sequence as: cited reference year, inventor's name, application or reissue status, and country of issuance.

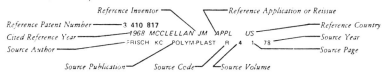

Reference Patent Number
Cited Reference Year
Source Author

Reference Inventor

Reference Application or Reissue

Reference Country
Source Year
Source Page

Source Publication   *Source Code*   *Source Volume*

Figure 6. This illustration, prepared by SCI's publisher, shows how to read entries in its Citation Index and its Source Entry Index. Patents are cited by number rather than name.

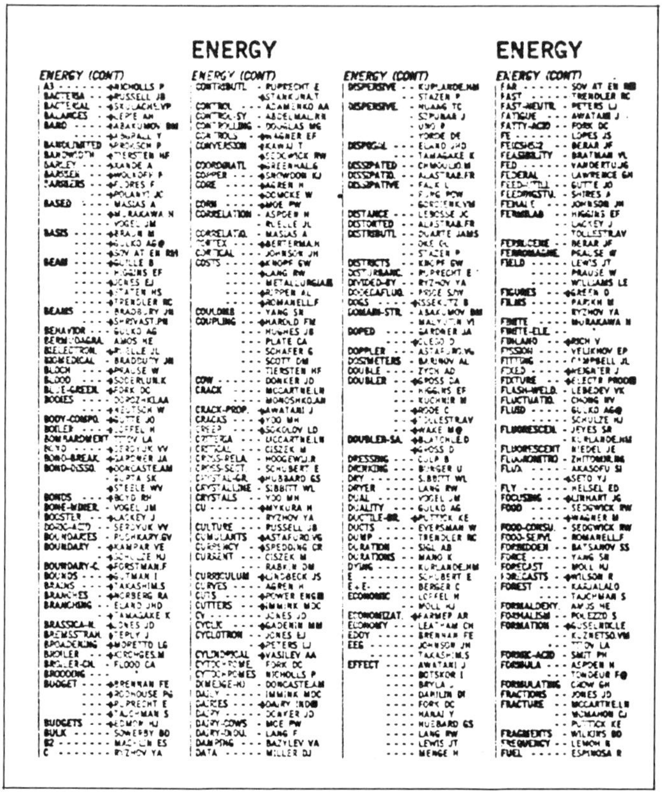

ENERGY

ENERGY

Figure 7. Sample entries from a page of SCI's Permuterm Index.

computer data bases. Several separate bases are currently available throughout the world. In order to use most of these, one need only have available a dedicated telephone line, (i.e., one that can be used exclusively and without interruption for this purpose) and some sort of output terminal—e.g., a teletype machine, an electric typewriter connected to an electronic decoder, or a videoscreen. They can be tapped into on a subscription or fee-for-services basis.[5]

Several information services are described briefly in Chapter 5 (beginning page 87). Data bases of the sort used by those services are summarized below, where one service is also more fully described.

The National Institute of Education's ERIC (Educational Resources Information Center) data base covers the literature of education and related subjects—e.g., library and information science, budgeting, automation, and administration. The ERIC data base includes information in the fields of career education, counseling services, the disadvantaged, early childhood education, exceptional children, higher education, reading and communication skills, instruction in various subject areas, teacher education, tests, measurement, evaluation, and many other topics. Its *Resources in Education* file indexes some 100,000 reports on funded education research, and its *Current Index to Journals in Education* covers articles from more than 500 education and education-related journals. In total, the ERIC data base contains about 400,000 citations with abstracts.

The American Psychological Association's Psychological Abstracts data base draws from more than 2000 periodicals and monographs published throughout the world. It indexes literature on all behavioral issues concerning humans or animals, and covers the fields of applied psychology, cognitive processes and motivation, communication, cultural influences and social issues, developmental and educational psychology, personality, physical and psychological disorders, and social behavior, among others. It contains almost 300,000 citations with abstracts, from 1967 to the present.

The MEDLARS data base is managed by the National Library of Medicine. It contains well over a million citations (without abstracts) from articles in some 3000 biomedical periodicals. Topics included are: human anatomy and physiology; animal and plant morphology and physiology; chemicals and drugs; analytical, diagnostic and therapeutic techniques and equipment; psychiatry and psychology; prevention and control of disease; biological and physical sciences; health care; nursing; veterinary medicine; the anthropological, educational, sociological, industrial, agricultural, and technical aspects of medicine; and the use of information science and communications in medicine.

(a)

BROWN RJ	BURRY RW	CAPUANO L	CEDERBAUM	CHATTOPADH
BROWN RJ C 4 SEE LORE JM BROWN SC 47 HEMLOCK CORNER, HENNIKER, NH, 03242, USA BROWSE NL C19 ST THOMAS HOSP & MED SCH, DEPT SURG, LONDON SE1 7EH, ENGLAND BRUCKNER R 111 SEE SCHOLZ H BRUN B 150 ST HANS HOSP, DEPT PSYCHOL, DK 4000 ROSKILDE, DENMARK BRUNEL Y 67 SEE RASSAT A BRUNNER H 62 UNIV REGENSBURG, INST CHEM, D 8400 REGENSBURG, FED REP GER BRUNNER HR C 5 CTR HOSP UNIV LAUSANNE, DEPT MED, CH 1011 LAUSANNE SWITZERLAND BRUYNINCKX WJ C 1 STATE UNIV GHENT, FAC DIERGENEESKUNDE, FYSIOL SCHEIKUNDE LAB, B 9000 GHENT, BELGIUM BRZOSKO W. C 1 MED ACAD WARSAW, INST INFECT & PARASIT DIS, DEPT IMMUNOPATHOL, PL 01201 WARSAW, POLAND BUCCHERI R 43 MAX PLANCK INST EXTRATERR PHYS, GARCHING MUNCHEN, FED REP GER BUCHANAN T C47 ROYAL VICTORIA HOSP,	BURRY RW 151 UNIV TENNESSEE, CTR HLTH SCI, DEPT ANAT, MEMPHIS, TN, 38163, USA BURTON BT C41 NIAMDD, PROGRAM ARTIFICIAL KIDNEY CHRON UREMIA, BETHESDA, MD 20014, USA BUSCARLET LA 164 CEN CADARACHE, CEA, DEPT BIOL, SERV RADIOAGRON, BP 1, F 13115 ST PAUL LEZ DURAN, FRANCE BUSHBY PA 163 MISSISSIPPI STATE UNIV, COLL VET MED, STATE COLLEGE, MS, 39762, USA BUSHELL GR 121 UNIV SYDNEY, ROYAL N SHORE HOSP, RAYMOND PURVES RES LABS, ST LEONARDS 2065, NEW S WALES, AUSTRALIA BUSUTTIL A C19 WESTERN GEN HOSP, DEPT PATHOL, EDINBURGH EH4 2XU, MIDLOTHIAN, SCOTLAND BUTLER TM 122 THOMAS JEFFERSON UNIV, DEPT PHYSIOL, PHILADELPHIA, PA, 19107, USA BUTT KMH C41 SUNY, DOWNSTATE MED CTR, DEPT SURG, BROOKLYN, NY, 11203, USA BUTTNERENNEVER J A 151 UNIV ZURICH, DEPT NEUROL, CH 8029 ZURICH, SWITZERLAND	CAPUANO L 74 UNIV SAARLAND, FACHBEREICH ORGAN CHEM 14, D 6600 SAARBRUCKEN, FED REP GER CARABELLO B C26 PETER BENT BRIGHAM HOSP, DIV CARDIOVASC CARDIOVASC SECT, BOSTON, MA, 02116, USA CARAMAZZA A 150 JOHNS HOPKINS UNIV, DEPT PSYCHOL, BALTIMORE, MD, 21218, USA CARAMAZZA A 155 JOHNS HOPKINS UNIV, DEPT PSYCHOL, BALTIMORE, MD, 21218, USA CARBONE A C32 1ST NAZL TUMORI, I, 20133 MILAN, ITALY CARDINAUD R 74 CENS, DEPT BIOL SERV BIOPHYS, F 91190 GIF SUR YVETTE, FRANCE CARERE A 106 IST SUPER SANITA, I 00161 ROME, ITALY CARLSON DE 122 JOHNS HOPKINS UNIV, SCH MED, DEPT BIOMED ENGN, BALTIMORE, MD, 21205, USA CARLSON SE 161 UNIV WISCONSIN, SCH MED, DEPT PATHOL, MADISON, WI, 53706, USA CARR HS 106 NEW YORK MED COLL, DEPT MICROBIOL, VALHALLA, NY, 10595, USA	CEDERBAUM AI 98 CUNY, MT SINAI SCH MED, DEPT BIOCHEM, NEW YORK, NY, 10029, USA CEFALO RC C 9 USN, NATL NAVAL MED CTR, KENNEDY INST BETHESDA, MD, 20014, USA CENTERWALL BS C 7 UNIV CALIF, SAN DIEGO, SCH MED, DEPT COMMUNITY MED, LA JOLLA, CA, 92093, USA CERFONTAIN H 53 UNIV AMSTERDAM, ORGAN CHEM LAB, AMSTERDAM 1004, NETHERLANDS CHABORA PC 48 CUNY, QUEENS COLL, DEPT BIOL, FLUSHING, NY 11367, USA CHALOUPKA J 145 CHARLES UNIV, FAC MED, INST PATHOPHYSIOL, CS 30599 PLZEN, CZECHOSLOVAKIA CHAMBAT G 93 CNRS, CNRS, MACROMOLEC VEGETALES RECH CTR, F 38041 GRENOBLE, FRANCE CHAMBERS KC 153 PORTLAND STATE UNIV, DEPT PSYCHOL, PORTLAND, OR, 97207 USA CHAMBERS RE 98 ROYAL INFIRM, DEPT CHEM PATHOL, BRISTOL BS2 8HW, ENGLAND CHAN NA 98 SEE FEIGELSON P CHAN V 129	CHATTOPADHYAY SP 109 UNIV BURDWAN, DEPT BOT, MICROBIOL LAB, BURDWAN 713101, W BENGAL, INDIA CHAVIS C 72 UNIV MONTPELLIER 2 CHIM BIOORGAN LAB, F 34060 MONTPELLIER FRANCE CHAYALO PP 131 ACAD MED SCI UKSSR INST GERONTOL, PATHOL PHYSIOL LAB, KIEV, UKSSR CHEETHAM NWH 93 UNIV NEW S WALES, SCH CHEM, KENSINGTON 2033, NEW S WALES, AUSTRALIA CHEMESOVA II 71 VL KOMAROV BOT INST LENINGRAD, USSR CHEN H 134 LOUISIANA STATE UNIV SCH MED CTR BIRTH DEFECTS, DEPT PEDIAT SHREVEPORT, LA, 71130 USA CHEN M C23 UNIV WASHINGTON, SCH MED, SEATTLE, WA, 98195, USA CHEN MC 98 SEE LORD RC CHEN WF 48 THOMAS JEFFERSON UNIV, DEPT SURG, PHILADELPHIA, PA, 19107 USA CHENOWETH PJ 157 COLORADO STATE UNIV, ANIM REPROD LAB, FT COLLINS, CO, 80523, USA CHEREST H 103 SEE SURDINKERJAN Y

Figure 8. Part of a page from Current Contents' *(a) author address directory, and (b) weekly subject index. Code numbers in (b) refer to* Current Contents *page where the* journal *contents page can be found, and the journal pages where articles begin.*

(b)

BETA-2		BINDIN		BIOSYN		BLEOMY		BLOOD-		BONE-S	
CC Pg	J Pg	CC Pg	J Pg	CC Pg	J Pg	CC Pg	J Pg	CC Pg	J Pg	CC Pg	J Pg

BETA-2-ADRENER GIC — C25 1008
BETA-2-AGONIST — C25 1001
BETAIN — 71 421
BETAMETHASON E-PHENOBARBI TAL-RITODRINE — C36 8
BETA2 — C25 985
BEWARE — 43 527
BEZAFIBRATE — 78 261
BF3.H2O-LIQUID — 59 2165
BHK-21-C13 — 91 349
BIAS — 150 673 / 675
BICARBONATE — 122 E 1 / E 22
BICYCLO[2.2.1]H EPT-2-ENE — 74 2646
BICYCLOBUTANE — 55 1475
BICYCLOBUTANE-1-CARBOXYLIC — 55 1475

BINDING-ACTIVIT Y — 48 830
BINDING-AFFINIT Y — 100 579
BINDING-PROPER TIES — 100 507
BINDING-SITE — 96 287
BINDING-SITES — 141 159 / 151 642
BIOACTIVITY — 113 53
BIOASSAY — 129 465
BIOAVAILABILITY — 39 233 / 63 887 / 117 5
BIOCHEMICAL — C11 1 / 107 1067 / 109 528 / 110 1 / 112 59 / 113 3 / 116 961 / 145 154 / 151 159
BIOCHEMICAL-AN ALYSIS — 105 11
BIOCHEMICAL-PR OPERTIES — 141 93

BIOSYNTHETICAL LY — 56 609
BIOTECHNOLOGY — 113 148
BIOTIN — 101 233
BIOTRANSFORMA TION — 116 899 / 904
BIPARIETAL — C28 487
BIPHENYL — 163 150 / 151
BIPHENYLS — 63 820 / 78 203
BIPLANE — C10 450
BIPOLAR — 121 31
BIRCH — C43 123
BIRD — 139 335
BIRTH-WEIGHT — C28 481 / 159 1522
BIS(ACETYL)TRIC ARBONYL(ETA-5-CYCLOPENTA DIENONE)BIS-(T RIPHENYLGERM YL)IRON — 59 2225

BLEOMYCIN — C30 1083
BLIGHT — 45 506
BLIND — C43 196
BLINDNESS — 155 51
BLOCH — 45 517
BLOCK — C.6 209 / C26 79 / C33 652
BLOCKADE — C47 151 / 236 / 122 H 46 / 129 535 / 141 105 / 319
BLOCKER — 101 507
BLOCKERS — 110 27
BLOCKING — 74 2586 / 96 143
BLOCKS — C23 664
BLOOD — C 1 313 / C10 463 / C19 143 / 184 / C28 495 / 500

BLOOD-PRESSURE — C 4 1 / C.7 315 / C35 273 / C39 88 / C48 441 / 115 441
BLOOD-PRESSURE E-PATIENTS — 136 141
BLOOD-PRESSURE E, ARTERIAL — 153 129
BLOOD-SAMPLES — 81 513
BLOOD-SERUM — 110 133
BLOOD-VESSEL — 48 857
BLOOD-VESSELS — 40 155 / 127 1
BLOOD-VOLUME — C39 88
BLOOD, HUMAN — 91 23
BLOOD, WHOLE — C1 314 / C46 213 / 106 359 / 126 37
BLUE — 68 1457 / 81 566 / 88 194

BONE-SCINTIGRA PHY — C11 111
BONES — 136 378 / 163 200
BOOSTER — 157 146
BORATE — 76 1268 / 81 668 / 109 517 / 528
BORATES — 78 197
BORERS — 46 630
BORNE — 140 31
BORON — 63 894 / 74 2469
BORON-NEUTRO N — 146 57
BORON-NITROGE N — 77 55
BOTTLING — 113 119
BOTULISM — 163 202
BOVINE — 48 831 / 52 555 / 85 83 / 88 1

The BIOSIS Previews data base contains citations available in *Biological Abstracts* and *Biological Abstracts/RRM*. About 140,000 items published in some 8000 serials, books, monographs, conference proceedings, and research communications, are annually added to the data base. Current citations are available in the data base about five weeks before they appear in the printed abstract; they cover fields such as microbiology, plant and animal sciences, biomedicine, agriculture, pharmacology, ecology, and other interdisciplinary areas such as biochemistry, bioengineering and biophysics.

The *New York Times* also maintains an Information Bank. It includes information indexed from the *New York Times* and 72 other significant magazines and newspapers. Its purpose is fast retrieval of current-events information in all important areas. It can also be used to retrieve general information and citations for specific research topics from a data base of about 2,000,000 citations and abstracts.

DIALOG: AN INFORMATION RETRIEVAL SERVICE EXEMPLIFIED

Lockheed describes its DIALOG as the world's leading on-line information system. It now includes more than 100 data base files—a total of about 30 million separate records. Access to the system is via virtually any "dial-up" (telecommunication-system linked) computer terminal. Thus it may be used at home, in the laboratory, in the office, or at the library. Available transmission speeds are 10, 15, 30, 120, and 480 characters per second, for bibliographic information, directories, or statistical data—all derived from data bases in science and technology, social sciences, arts, humanities, business, finance, current affairs, and the media. Information searches made via DIALOG are typically faster and more inclusive than manual searches, and cost only about one fifth as much to run—electronic time is, in this instance, more efficient and cheaper than human labor.

DIALOG can provide an abstract or cite bibliographic details. It can also simply list the number of citations in its files that could reply to a query given it. Records available are from: books, periodicals, reports, descriptions of current research, dissertations, patents, conference proceedings, bibliographies, pamphlets, manuals, monographs, legislative documents, reviews, newspaper articles, notes, nonprint media, correspondence, and lectures. Full texts of cited items may be ordered and billed on-line. Updated information can be requested on standing order for continuing responses to questions. In any given time zone, file availability is about 100 hours each week, always for a minimal cost. Training/start up is easy.

Other features include: selection on the basis of any subject term, name of person, place, or organization; Boolean combination of terms to narrow or broaden search output; browsing for related subject terms; searching for specific character strings—a specific term, a phrase, several terms in close juxtaposition in a particular record, or terms that have a common root (for example, to search *library, libraries, librarian* on one command); return to previous search results, even after changing data bases, and the ability to store the search logic for re-searching after many weeks or months; and, an optional search restriction to particular categories—say, subject heading, title, or author.

As an example of DIALOG coverage, areas that might be addressed in searching the chemical and related literature included in the more than 30 relevant data bases on file are: food and agriculture, forest products, textiles, mining, metal products, environment, pollution, energy, toxicology, pest control and pesticides, mathematics, physics, pharmaceuticals, geochemistry, chemical engineering, alloys, polymers, coordination compounds, government regulations, patents, equivalent patents, Chemical Abstracts (CA) service registry numbers, CA index names, and chemical name synonyms. Searched items might include: registry number and index names, related nomenclature terms and segmentation, chemical name synonyms, molecular formula, element counts, periodic index terms, ring data, general and related subject and index headings, index modification words, keyword phrases, titles, corporate sources, patent assignees and numbers, corresponding patents, and language and patent limits.

Similar profiles might be drawn for any other disciplines and sub-specialties. DIALOG continues to add new records and new kinds of items, as well as entire data bases so that the system continues to grow in depth and breadth.

CROSS-REFERENCES

Under the headings you check, you will sometimes be instructed to look under another heading (see Figure 5, p. 52). Add these new cross-referenced headings to your list as they are uncovered and search accordingly.

Some abstracts may use a KWIC (Key-Word-In-Context) subject index to provide a quick entry into the subject content of the abstracts. One or more keyword entries are derived for each abstract from the title, text, or context of the abstract (see Figure 9). Use your dictionary to identify related terms, then check other subject-related abstracts and reviews for articles and other printed sources of information. Indexed articles are usually listed by subject or by author and title. In some indexes, every author's name appearing on the original article is listed alphabetically in the author index, including corporate authors for organizational or society reports. Most give the following data: title of article, author, periodical title, volume number, inclusive paging, and date of issue. Listed alphabetically are the periodical titles that are regularly indexed. Usually, the information is given in abbreviated form.

INDEXES TO DISSERTATIONS AND THESES FROM ACADEMIC INSTITUTIONS

Each year doctoral candidates in leading colleges and universities throughout the world make significant contributions to human understanding and knowledge by means of their doctoral dissertations. Since 1938, an index to this great wealth of useful knowledge has been published by University Microfilms on microfilm and in *Dissertation Abstracts International (DAI)*[6], listing 30,000 new abstracts yearly. The development of xerography in the 1950s made it possible to obtain dissertation copies on paper or microfilm.

Doctoral degree candidates and library searchers in all fields can now use an information retrieval system, DATRIX (Direct Access to Reference Information: A Xerox Service), developed by University Microfilms. DATRIX searches the entire *DAI* file for dissertations relevant to a particular subject.

Comprehensive Dissertations Index (CDI), 1861–1972, is an attempt to list all dissertations accepted at universities in the United States and some from Canada and other countries. It is an index of authors and keywords. The *DAI* citation number and page is shown after the name of the degree-granting institution; finally, the University Microfilms publication number is shown for dissertations available on microfilm from that supplier. *CDI* is divided into these broad areas:

Volumes 1–4	Chemistry
Volume 5	Mathematics and Statistics
Volume 6	Astronomy and Physics
Volume 7	Physics
Volume 8	General and Aeronautical Engineering
Volume 9	Chemical, Mechanical, and Metallurgical Engineering
Volume 10	Civil, Electrical, and Industrial Engineering

KIDNEY · KINETICS

Subject Context	Keyword	Ref. No.
MPLEX VIRUS THYMIDINE	KINASE EXPRESSION IN INFECTION OF TH	58718
UVATE PYRO PHOSPHATE	FIELD GROWTH CHAMBER/ BIOCH	60530
ROM BOVINE SERUM URO	FLUFENAMATE HEMATOLOGIC-DR	55531
INOGEN ACTIVATOR URO	FROM CULTURED CELLS HUMAN	55533
NOL PYRUVATE CARBOXY	FRUCTOSE 1 6 DI PHOSPHATASE	56428
NOL PYRUVATE CARBOXY	FUMARASE MALATE FORMATION	60528
MAN SERUM URINE HEXO	GLUCOSE OXIDASE OXYGEN RATE	55383
ATE CREATINE PHOSPHO	GLUTAMIC OXAL ACETIC TRANS A	58840
AND ADP TO CARBAMATE	GLUTAMINE SYNTHETASE AND CA	60188
TRANSFERASE GLYCERO	GLYCERO PHOSPHATE ACYL TRA	60497
YDROGENASE PYRUVATE	GLYCOLYSIS/ EFFECT OF ELECTRI	58876
TREPTO KINASE AND URO	HUMAN THROMBIN/ INFLUENCE	55534
DEHYDROGENASE HEXO	HYBRIDIZATION ISO ELECTRIC FO	58534
ARTERY ACETYL CHOLINE	II PROSTAGLANDIN PHARMACO KI	61722
KINASE DEOXY CYTIDINE	IMMUNE DYS FUNCTION TOXICITY	58088
MP DEPENDENT PROTEIN	IN NORMAL AND GOITROUS RAT T	57304
HROMBOLYSIS WITH URO	IN RABBITS HUMAN LEUKOCYTE F	59710
NE ON THYROIDAL FUCO	IN RATS HUMAN HORMONE-DRUG/ EFFEC	57324
LOCK PHOSPHO FRUCTO	INHIBITION/ METABOLIC FATE OF	58304
UMAN SERUM CREATINE	ISO ENZYME MB MYO CARDIAL IN	55897
DOGS HUMAN CREATINE	ISO ENZYME MB/ DIAGNOSIS OF	55975
OF THE RAT ADENYLATE	ISOZYMES EC-2 7 4 3 RATTUS-NO	57739
EPHOSPHO COENZYME A	KINETICS/ MITOCHONDRIAL BIOSY	57401
METABOLIC-DRUG HEXO	LACTATE DEHYDROGENASE PHOS	59922
DING GENETIC CREATINE	LACTATE DEHYDROGENASE PYRU	55144
RUM CREATINE PHOSPHO	LIGHT MICROSCOPY LEAKAGE/ A	58839
ICAL METHODS CREATINE	LIPASE ASPARTATE AMINO TRANS	55359
NYLATE KINASE ACETATE	N N' METHYLENE BIS ACRYLAMID	57414
P INDEPENDENT PROTEIN	ONCORNAVIRUS RABBIT IMMUNO	57595
SCULAR-DRUG THROMBO	OXYGEN CONSUMPTION ORGAN	59634
INASE PHOSPHO FRUCTO	PHOSPHO CREATINE ASPARTATE	59403
OSE 6 PHOSPHATE HEXO	PHOSPHO FRUCTO KINASE CARB	61747
ERGY PHOSPHATES HEXO	PHOSPHO FRUCTO KINASE PHOS	59403
DIABETIC RABBITS HEXO	PHOSPHO GLUCO MUTASE GLUC	57179
LASE A PHOSPHORYLASE	PHOSPHORYLASE PHOSPHATASE	59362
D RNA INDUCED PROTEIN	PHOSPHORYLATE THE SAME SITE	58773
NASE PHOSPHO FRUCTO	PYRUVATE LACTATE AGE PHARM	59922
F THROMBOLYSIS BY URO	RABBIT HUMAN LIVER KIDNEY PH	59611
F THE CALVES CREATINE	SEX/ SPINAL MUSCULAR ATROPH	58841
EIN DERIVATIVE STREPTO	STREPTODORNASE LYMPHOKINE	58102
PID DEPENDENT PROTEIN	SYSTEM RAT BRAIN PHOSPHATID	57334
IONS ON THE CREATINE	SYSTEMS OF MYO CARDIAL CELLS	57395
N TRANSLATION PROTEIN	TERNARY COMPLEX GDP METHO	57739
DIATOR DEOXY CYTIDINE	THYMIDINE SENSITIVITY SPONTAN	59242
A-FM 3A CELL THYMIDINE	THYMIDYLATE KINASE DNA SYNT	57672
DROGENASE ADENYLATE	UDP PYRO PHOSPHATASE UDP G	57179
ANTI PLASMIN STREPTO	URO KINASE/ A NEW DETERMINA	55528
MENT ASSOCIATING URO	WITH HEPARIN HUMAN CARDIOVA	59667
3 PHOSPHO GLYCERATE	2 EC-2 7 2.3 FROM THE MOUSE	57688
MP DEPENDENT PROTEIN	KINASES BY VASOACTIVE INTESTINAL PEP	59730
ATUS EGGS METABOLISM	CYCLIC AMP DEPENDENT IONOP	58350
ERYTHROCYTE PROTEIN	RABBIT HEART BOVINE CEREBRA	55498
MP DEPENDENT PROTEIN	STUDIES ON HUMAN ERYTHROC	55498
TRAINING PROGRAM ON	KINDERGARTEN CHILDREN ROSNER RICH	60969
NYTOIN ON AMYGDALOID	KINDLED RAT EPILEPTIC FOCUS AMYGDAL	59345
L SPIKING IN THE AWAKE	SEIZURES IN THE RAT HUMAN A	58279
UENCE OF HIPPOCAMPAL	KINDLING ON SLEEP ORGANIZATION IN C	60964
G CENTRAL DEPRESSANT	TECHNIQUE STIMULATION/ EFF	60964
ED INHERITANCE HUMAN	KINDRED PEDIGREE/ ELEVATED THYROXI	57841
GENETIC COUNSELING/ A	WITH CASES OF 4P TRISOMY AN	57828
PONENTS/ ACUTE HYPER	KINESIA AFTER HYPOTHALAMIC LESIONS	59310
VEL AND TYPE OF HYPER	INDUCED BY VENTROMEDIAL AN	59310
IN EXPERIMENTAL HYPO	RAT CATECHOLAMINE SUCCINIC	57020
KULL BILL/ THE ROLE OF	KINESIS AND MECHANICAL ADVANTAGE I	56191
NGS OF CHILDREN HYPER	BEHAVIOR DISORDER AGGRESSIV	60826
BLOOD POOL SCAN HYPER	CORONARY ARTERY DISEASE/ TH	55911
TIINFLAMMATORY CHEMO	HUMAN ASYNERGY RADIO NUCLI	55998
EARNING LIGHT SHADOW	IMMUNE COMPLEXES/ MIGRATIO	58147
A-OVIS DEVELOPMENT OF	KINESTHETIC TACTILE STIMULI CHOICE S	55207
KIDNEY CORTEX SLICES A	KINETES IN THE GUT OF THE VECTOR TIC	55944
OLI ANTIBIOTIC ACTIVITY	KINETIC ANALYSIS ACETATE METABOLIC-D	61790
NE PHARMACO KINETICS/	ANALYSIS ENZYME/ SYNTHESIS	56063
R CELL POPULATIONS BY	ANALYSIS OF THE INTERACTION	59917
ILLUS-SUBTILIS PR-70 1	AND MONO LAYER ADSORPTION	58100
FJORD EQUILIBRIUM AND	BEHAVIOR OF SOLUBILIZED ENZY	57614
N IN NEURONAL UPTAKE	CONSIDERATIONS BACTERIA BRIT	56756
LACTAM ANTIBIOTICS 3	EVIDENCE FOR CO TRANSPORT R	59917
IN PHARMACO KINETICS/	EVIDENCE FOR IN-SITU ABSORPT	56170
/ EFFECTS OF THE ADIPO	EVIDENCE FOR MULTIPLE CHEMI	61677
RACY PREGNANCY TEST/	HORMONE ON THE RELEASE AND	58310
NCE TREATMENT/ HYPER	IMMUNO TURBIDIMETRY THE ME	61264
LAR VERGENCE/ THE SYN	IMPULSE DISORDER A DEVELOPM	60850
	INTERACTION OF CONVERGENCE	61373

Subject Context	Keyword	Ref. No.
MONE-DRUG	PHARMACO	KINETICS /DISTRIBUTION AND METABOLIS	59817
E INTESTINE	PHARMACO	DISTRIBUTION OF TRITIUM LA	59831
ATOGRAPHY	PHARMACO	/DO NEUROLEPTICS PREVENT T	61719
AVAILABILITY	PHARMACO	/DRUG NONEQUIVALENCE B. SO	59790
CODYNAMICS	PHARMACO	/DRUG NONEQUIVALENCE 9 RE	59763
NOMIC-DRUG	PHARMACO	/DUAL HISTAMINE RECEPTOR M	60085
-DRUG RENIN	PHARMACO	/EFFECT OF CHRONIC TREATME	60005
DIUM WATER	PHARMACO	/EFFECT OF INDOMETHACIN ON	61654
CODYNAMICS	PHARMACO	/EFFECT OF MOLECULAR STRUC	59731
US ACTIVITY	PHARMACO	/EFFECT OF ORAL LABETALOL O	59679
HYDROPENIA	PHARMACO	/EFFECT OF PHLORIZIN ON REN	60103
ER HALF-LIFE	PHARMACO	/EFFECT OF PROBENECID ON C	59217
CODYNAMICS	PHARMACO	/EFFECT OF PROCAINAMIDE ON	59640
MONE-DRUG	PHARMACO	/EFFECTS OF ACUTE HYPOTENS	59641
SFORMATION	PHARMACO	/EFFECTS OF ALLOPURINOL ON	59782
O RECEPTOR	PHARMACO	/EFFECTS OF ANGIOTENSIN II	61721
CODYNAMICS	PHARMACO	/EFFECTS OF ANTI INFLAMMATO	59738
ION VOLUME	PHARMACO	/EFFECTS OF CARBAMAZEPINE	59965
HEART RATE	PHARMACO	/EFFECTS OF METOPROLOL ON	59697
INTERACTION	PHARMACO	/EFFECTS OF PRE TREATMENT	61720
S HISTOLOGY	PHARMACO	/EFFECTS OF RIBOFLAVINE ON	61671
CODYNAMICS	PHARMACO	/ENHANCEMENT OF MACROPHA	59775
LINICAL USE	PHARMACO	/ESTIMATION OF KINETIC PARA	59781
MONE-DRUG	PHARMACO	/ESTROGEN DEPENDENT DIFFER	56136
OF PROPOLIS	PHARMACO	/EYE MEDICINAL FILMS WITH A	60093
NOMIC-DRUG	PHARMACO	/FOOD INDUCED REDUCTION IN	59964
TOLERANCE	PHARMACO	/FORMATION OF ALPHA METHY	60684
RENCE NAD	DEPENDENT	/GENETIC CONTROL OF RESPON	57710
GLUCONO-1	5 LACTONE	/GLUCOSE OXIDASE EC-1 1.3.4	58313
CATALYTIC	MECHANISM	/GLUTAMYL TRANSFER RNA SY	57554
ASITIC-DRUG	PHARMACO	/HIGH PERFORMANCE LIQUID C	56123
V DETECTOR	PHARMACO	/HIGH PRESSURE LIQUID CHRO	59811
YDROGENASE	PHARMACO	/HOMOGENOUS ENZYMO IMMU	59969
S METHYL GLUTATHIONE		/HYDROLYSIS OF GLUTATHIONE	56456
CODYNAMICS	PHARMACO	/IN-VIVO ABSORPTION OF PHEN	59962
CODYNAMICS	PHARMACO	/IN-VIVO DIRECT EFFECTS OF	59664
ACTURE AGE	PHARMA	/INHIBITION OF FRACTURE HEA	61678
INTERACTION	PHARMACO	/INTERACTION BETWEEN AMITRI	61735
ANOL WATER	PHARMACO	/INTERACTION OF DOXANTRAZO	59864
MAN SERUM	PHARMACO	/INTERACTION OF LOCAL ANEST	59938
ATOGRAPHY	PHARMACO	/INTERFERENCE OF CEFOXITIN	56148
HOTOMETRY	PHARMACO	/INTRA INDIVIDUAL SIMILARIT	60008
OMETHAMINE	PHARMACO	/IONIZATION KINETICS OF THE	59618
ATE PROTEIN	INTERACTION	/ISOLATION CHARACTERIZATION	59917
ATION RATIO	PHARMACO	/KINETIC ANALYSIS OF THE IN	59917
TEINS URINE	PHARMACO	/KINETIC EVIDENCE FOR MULTI	61677
YS FUNCTION	PHARMACO	/KINETICS OF DIGESTIVE ENZY	59839
RESTRICTION	PHARMACO	/MASS SPECTROMETRY OF CHL	59249
ACER STUDY	PHARMACO	/MECHANISM RESPONSIBLE FO	59835
ITIS THERAPY	PHARMACO	/METABOLIC ABNORMALITIES O	57006
YDROGENASE	PHARMACO	/METABOLIC FATE OF A NEW A	59976
MR ANALYSIS	PHARMACO	/METABOLISM OF GOLD IN THE	59721
ECTROMETRY	PHARMACO	/METABOLISM IN N ACETYL PR	60088
REDUCTASE	PHARMACO	/METABOLISM OF PROTRIPTYLIN	60007
RESISTANCE	PHARMACO	/METABOLISM OF THE NEW PSY	60038
HO COENZYME A	KINASE	/METABOLISM OF TRITIUM LABE	60080
NOMIC-DRUG	PHARMACO	/METABOLISM OF 2 PROSTAGLA	59827
INFARCTION	PHARMACO	/MITOCHONDRIAL BIOSYNTHESI	57401
CODYNAMICS	PHARMACO	/MODIFICATIONS OF CENTRAL 5	60048
TE RANDOM	MECHANISM	/MODULATION OF LIPOLYTIC AC	61724
ION TOXICITY	PHARMACO	/MONO HYDROXY TAMOXIFEN A	60064
ECTROMETRY	PHARMACO	/MULTI FUNCTIONALITY OF LIV	57391
ABOLIC-DRUG	PHARMACO	/MULTIPLE DOSE AMIKACIN SER	56156
NAL DISEASE	PHARMACO	/MULTIPLE FORMS OF NONINDU	61642
CODYNAMICS	PHARMACO	/MULTIPLE SEROTONIN RECEPT	59923
CODYNAMICS	PHARMACO	/NAPHTHOXY LACTIC-ACID AFTE	59685
CODYNAMICS	PHARMACO	/NEUROLEPTIC RECEPTORS STE	60056
CODYNAMICS	PHARMACO	/NEW ANTI ARRHYTHMIC AGEN	59689
CODYNAMICS	PHARMACO	/NEW ANTI ARRHYTHMIC AGEN	59690
CODYNAMICS	PHARMACO	/NEW ANTI ARRHYTHMIC AGEN	59691
HLOROFORM	PHARMACO	/NONAQUEOUS METHOD FOR E	59853
OGENASES	IMMUNOLOGY	/OXIDATION OF MALATE BY ISO	60622
EMO GLOBIN	PHARMACO	/OXYGEN TRANSPORT DURING	61662
ABSORPTION	PHARMACO	/PARACETAMOL METABOLISM I	59772
R INHIBITION	PHARMACO	/PHARMACOLOGICAL SCREENIN	59838
HEART RATE	PHARMACO	/PLASMA LEVELS AND BETA BL	59702
L STIMULANT	PHARMACO	/PLASMA LEVELS OF CHLORIMIP	60025
UTIC LEVELS	PHARMACO	/PLASMA PROLACTIN DURING T	61697
STAGLANDIN	PHARMACO	/PLASMA THEOPHYLLINE LEVEL	60087
TOLERANCE	PHARMACO	/POTENTIATION OF THE ALGOG	61722
E SCATCHARD	ANALYSIS	/PRE TREATMENT WITH DELTA-	60678
ARRHYTHMIC	PHARMACO	/PRESENCE OF 1 ESSENTIAL AR	57390
		/PRILOCAINE EFFECT ON ACONI	59622

Figure 9. Part of a page from the subject index of Biological Abstracts *showing one use of key words for indexed entry into subject matter of the literature.*

Volume 11	Biology and Zoology
Volume 12	Anatomy, Physiology, and Genetics
Volume 13	Botany, Microbiology, and Bacteriology
Volume 14	Health and Environmental Sciences
Volume 15	Agriculture
Volume 16	Geography and Geology
Volume 17	Social Sciences
Volumes 18–19	Psychology
Volumes 20–24	Education
Volumes 25–26	Business and Economics
Volume 27	Law and Political Science
Volume 28	History
Volumes 29–30	Language and Literature
Volume 31	Communication and the Arts
Volume 32	Philosophy and Religion
Volumes 33–37	Author Index

An annual supplement has been issued since 1973 updating the original volumes.

Figure 10 is a sample page from *CDI*. After you select the more promising titles and citations from this index, turn to volume-issue and page in *DAI* to read the dissertation abstract. If more information is needed, order a microfilm copy of the entire dissertation from University Microfilms.

GOVERNMENT DOCUMENTS

Government documents and government publications include reports, bulletins, and publications issued by a municipal, state, or federal agency. The *U.S. Government Organization Manual* (Washington, D.C., U.S.G.P.O., 1935–) contains an appendix listing more than 150 important periodicals published on a regular basis by different departments and agencies of the federal government. For an overview of the breadth and scope of federal publications, see L. F. Schmeckebier's *Government Publications and Their Use* (1969, Brookings Institute, Washington, D.C.), and *U.S. Government Serials and Periodicals* (1972, Documents Index, McLean, VA).

To find government publications, consult the indexed *Monthly Catalog of United States Government Publications* (Washington, D.C., U.S.G.P.O., 1895–), the major index to U.S. government publications. Until 1976, each December issue carried a cumulated index of the 20,000 new documents listed each year. This index is now issued separately, semi-annually.

Two other indexes provide easy access to federal government publications: the *Congressional Information Service (CIS) Index*, and

64 RESEARCH

ABORTIVE
MECHANISMS OF COLICIN ACTION AND OF ABORTIVE
INFECTION BY BACTERIOPHAGE— FIELDS, KAY
LOUISE (PH D 1968 MASSACHUSETTS INSTITUTE OF
TECHNOLOGY) X1968, p 23

ABSCISSION
INFLUENCE OF GROWTH REGULATORS UPON THE
CORRELATIVE MOBILIZATION AND ABSCISSION
PROCESSES OF THE PRIMARY LEAVES OF
PHASEOLUS VULGARIS L — KADKADE, PRAKASH
GOPAL (PH D 1970 SAINT LOUIS UNIVERSITY) 231p
31/08 B, p 4511   71–03270
TUMBLEWEEDS ECOLOGY AND ABSCISSION— BECKER,
DONALD AUGUST (PH D 1968 THE UNIVERSITY OF
NORTH DAKOTA) 153p 29/11 B, p 4040   69–08532

ABSORBANCE
BETA-CAROTENE INVOLVEMENT AND THE POSSIBILITY
OF A MEMBRANE POTENTIAL ASSOCIATED WITH THE
520NM ABSORBANCE CHANGE— STRICHARTZ, GARY
RICHARD (PH D 1970 UNIVERSITY OF
PENNSYLVANIA) 187p 31/11 B, p 6445   71–07864

ABSORBED
ISODENSITOMETRIC EVALUATION OF ABSORBED DOSE
RATES IN GROWING AND ADULT FELINE BONE
RESULTING FROM CONTINUOUS EXPOSURE TO LOW
LEVELS OF STRONTIUM 90— ROSENSTEIN,
LAURENCE (PH D 1970 UNIVERSITY OF CINCINNATI)
123p 31/07 B, p 3856   71–01134

ABSORPTION
GROWTH AND MINERAL ABSORPTION BY TRIGONELLA
FOENUM-GRAECUM SEEDLINGS FROM SEEDS
WASHED FOLLOWING GAMMA-IRRADIATION—
FREEMAN, JANICE RAYE (PH D 1971 TEXAS
WOMAN'S UNIVERSITY) X1971, p 32
NEAR ULTRAVIOLET CIRCULAR DICHROISM AND
ABSORPTION SPECTRA OF PHENYLALANINE,
TYROSINE AND RIBONUCLEASE A AT 298 AND 77
DEGREES K— HORWITZ, JOSEPH (PH D 1970
UNIVERSITY OF CALIFORNIA, LOS ANGELES) 149p
31/04 B, p 1747   70–19855
ION AND CARBOHYDRATE ABSORPTION IN THE
POSTERIOR INTESTINE OF CRYPTOCHITON
STELLERI— PUDDY, ROBERT EARL (PH D 1970
UNIVERSITY OF HOUSTON) 106p 31/05 B, p 2487
                                        70–22328
ABSORPTION D AMINO-ACIDES PAR L INTESTIN ISOLE
DE LA GRENOUILLE, RANA PIPIENS— DE LA NOUE,
JOEL (PH D 1969 UNIVERSITE LAVAL (CANADA))
X1969, p 27
SEMI-EMPIRICAL SELF CONSISTENT FIELD MOLECULAR
ORBITAL CALCULATIONS ON THE ELECTRONIC
STRUCTURE AND ABSORPTION SPECTRA OF 1,4-, 1,6-,
AND 1 2 DIHYDRONICOTINAMIDES— MAGGIORA,
GERALD MAURICE (PH D 1968 UNIVERSITY OF
CALIFORNIA, DAVIS) 152p 30/04 B, p 1527
                                        69–16362
THE RELATION OF THE INTRACELLULAR ABSORPTION
OF ANTIGEN TO THE PRODUCTION OF ANTIBODY—
COOK, MARJORIE WESTON (PH D 1919 BROWN
UNIVERSITY) S0024

ABSORPTIVE
STUDIES ON THE MORPHOLOGY, FUNCTION, AND
PHYLOGENETIC IMPLICATIONS OF THE
ACANTHOCEPHALAN ABSORPTIVE SURFACE—
BYRAM, JAMES EDWARD, III (PH D 1971 RICE
UNIVERSITY) 202p 32/04-B, p 2006   71–26265

ACANTHAMOEBA
RIBOSOMAL RNA SYNTHESIS DURING ENCYSTMENT IN
ACANTHAMOEBA CASTELLANII NEFF— BIGGS, MAY
K (PH D 1971 THE CATHOLIC UNIVERSITY OF
AMERICA) 64p 32/04-B p 2005   71–25244
AN ANALYSIS OF THE CHEMISTRY AND FUNCTION OF
MICROTUBULE PROTEIN AS RELATED TO CELL
DIVISION IN ACANTHAMOEBA RHYSODES— RUBIN,
ROBERT WARD (PH D 1971 MICHIGAN STATE
UNIVERSITY) 156p 32/09-B p 5037   72–08774
THE ENVIRONMENTAL CONTROL OF CYTOCHROME
OXIDASE ACTIVITY IN ACANTHAMOEBA
CASTELLANII— RUDICK, MICHAEL JAY (PH D 1970
THE OHIO STATE UNIVERSITY) 72p 31/07 B p 3857
                                        70–26355
CELL SIZE AND MACROMOLECULE COMPOSITION
DURING AGING IN CULTURES OF ACANTHAMOEBA
CASTELLANII— RUDICK, VICTORIA LOUISE WATERS
(PH D 1969 THE OHIO STATE UNIVERSITY) 90p
30 10 B p 4509   70–06867

ACANTHOCEPHALAN
STUDIES ON THE MORPHOLOGY, FUNCTION, AND
PHYLOGENETIC IMPLICATIONS OF THE
ACANTHOCEPHALAN ABSORPTIVE SURFACE—
BYRAM, JAMES EDWARD, III (PH D 1971 RICE
UNIVERSITY) 202p 32/04-B, p 2006   71–26265

ACANTHOPARYPHIUM
NEUROSECRETION IN THE LIFE CYCLE OF THE
DIGENETIC TREMATODE, ACANTHOPARYPHIUM
SPINULOSUM, JOHNSTON, 1917— STEELE, DAVID
FREED (PH D 1970 UNIVERSITY OF SOUTHERN
CALIFORNIA) 97p 32/01-B p 93   71–16437

ACARINA
THE DIVERSITY OF CELL TYPES IN THE
NEUROSECRETORY SYSTEM OF THE AMERICAN DOG
TICK, DERMACENTOR VARIABILIS, SAY (ACARINA,
IXODIDAE)— OBENCHAIN, FREDERICK DECROES (PH D
1970 THE OHIO STATE UNIVERSITY) 102p 32/01-B,
p 89   71–18063

ACCLIMATION
TEMPERATURE ACCLIMATION IN MARINE INTERTIDAL
PROSOBRANCH MOLLUSCS— HAMBY, ROBERT J
(PH D 1970 UNIVERSITY OF CHICAGO) X1970, p 26
EFFECTS OF THERMAL AND OSMOTIC ACCLIMATION
ON AN ESTUARINE GASTROPOD— MCRITCHIE,
ROBERT GERALD (PH D 1968 RICE UNIVERSITY) 71p
29/07-B, p 2297   68–15642

ACER
AN ELECTROPHORETIC AND SEROLOGICAL STUDY OF
INTRAGENERIC VARIATION IN THE GENUS ACER
(ACERACEAE) OF EASTERN NORTH AMERICA—
ZIEGENFUS, THEODORE THOMAS (PH D 1970 WEST
VIRGINIA UNIVERSITY) 77p 31/08-B, p 4523
                                        71–04858
REGULATION OF RESPIRATION AND GLYCOLYSIS IN
CULTURED CELLS OF ACER PSEUDOPLATANUS L —
GIVAN, CURTIS VAN DUSEN (PH D 1968 HARVARD
UNIVERSITY) X1968, p 23

ACERACEAE
AN ELECTROPHORETIC AND SEROLOGICAL STUDY OF
INTRAGENERIC VARIATION IN THE GENUS ACER
(ACERACEAE) OF EASTERN NORTH AMERICA—
ZIEGENFUS, THEODORE THOMAS (PH D 1970 WEST
VIRGINIA UNIVERSITY) 77p 31/08-B, p 4523
                                        71–04858

ACESTRORHYNCHINI
SYSTEMATICS AND EVOLUTION OF THE TRIBE
ACESTRORHYNCHINI (PISCES CHARACIDAE)—
MENEZES, NAERCIO AQUINO (PH D 1968 HARVARD
UNIVERSITY) X1968, p 23

ACETABULAR
THE FINE STRUCTURE OF THE ACETABULAR
SECRETORY GLANDS OF THE CERCARIAE OF
SCHISTOSOMA MANSONI— DORSEY, CHARLES
HERBERT (PH D 1971 HOWARD UNIVERSITY) 140p
32/11 B, p 6214   72–14033

ACETABULARIA
THE CONTROL OF PROTEIN SYNTHESIS DURING THE
DIFFERENTIATION OF ACETABULARIA— CERON,
GABRIEL (PH D 1969 THE UNIVERSITY OF FLORIDA)
107p 31/03-B p 1074   70–14863

ACETI
RIBITOL SYNTHESIS IN TURBATRIX ACETI—
PANAGIDES, JOHN (PH D 1972 STATE UNIVERSITY
OF NEW YORK AT BUFFALO) X1972

ACETYLCHOLINE
BLOCKADE OF ACETYLCHOLINE RECEPTORS BY COBRA
TOXIN ELECTROPHYSIOLOGY AND
PHARMACOLOGY— LESTER HENRY ALLEN (PH D
1971 THE ROCKEFELLER UNIVERSITY) 128p 32/12 B
p 6856   72–16994

ACETYLCHOLINESTERASE
REGENERATION OF VENTRAL ROOTS INTO THE DORAL
HORN AND AXOPLASMIC FLOW OF
ACETYLCHOLINESTERASE— RANISH, NORMAN ALAN
(PH D 1972 INDIANA UNIVERSITY AT INDIANAPOLIS)
X1972, p 35
THE LACK OF PHOSPHAMIDASE ACTIVITY IN
ACETYLCHOLINESTERASE— WHALEN, THOMAS
ALOYSIUS (PH D 1969 NEW YORK UNIVERSITY) 69p
30, 06 B p 2550   69–21280

Figure 10. Part of a page from CDI.

the *American Statistics Index*. The *CIS Index* is a vital reference resource because Congressional publications are among the most current, detailed, and authoritative reference resources available in some fields. The U.S. Congress examines a broad variety of subjects in great detail, and publishes primary information representing a wide range of viewpoints and expertise. *The American Statistics Index (ASI)* is a guide to the masses of statistical data produced by the U.S. Government. *ASI* covers more than 400 individual agencies that issue statistical data. It indexes all data currently collected by the government on a particular subject. Both the *CIS Index* and *ASI* furnish original documents on microfiches.

Publications of some states, other countries, and international organizations may be located in the Main Card Catalog. Also consult the *Monthly Checklist of State Publications* (Washington, D.C., U.S.G.P.O., 1910– , which records all state publications received by the Library of Congress.

Publications of the United Nations and its specialized agencies are listed in the *United Nations Documents Index*, issued monthly and including two separate annual cumulations: *The Cumulative Checklist* and *The Cumulative Index* (New York, United Nations Publications, v. 1- , 1950–). For documents prior to 1950 see the United Nations, Secretariat, Department of Public Information, Library Services, *Checklist of United Nations Documents* (Lake Success, New York, 1949).

OBTAINING GOVERNMENT DOCUMENTS

Once you have references to a government publication, how can you obtain the document?

Ideally, you get on a federal mailing list for a given publication series. You can be included on "initial distribution" lists by, for example, (*a*) receiving a government contract or grant in a subject field; (*b*) requesting the publications from the responsible office in the issuing agency (with written justification for your request); or (*c*) being a member library in the Federal Depository Library Program. However, most of us obtain federal documents via "secondary distribution." Unless you have a sympathetic congressman (they all have quotas on government documents for free distribution) or request only a few documents of the right person in the correct agency, this means you purchase document services.

The Superintendent of Documents (SoD) tends to handle large-volume sales items. SoD sells through mail orders and government bookstores more than 27,000 different "in print" (Knox, 1972, p. 6) government publications. Sales are based primarily on listings in the

Monthly Catalog and selected *Price Lists*, assembled from time to time for documents in a given or several related subject areas. The *Monthly Catalog* and *Price Lists* may be obtained free of charge. Printings are often small, so many documents quickly fall "out of print."

The National Technical Information Service (NTIS) is probably the world's largest specialty publisher. It sells over 750,000 different documents published since about 1950 by hundreds of organizations, mainly federal government agencies. For example, through the Council on Environmental Quality, NTIS receives and makes available to the public all *Environmental Impact Statements*. Documents from the Environmental Protection Agency (EPA), the National Oceanographic and Atmospheric Administration (NOAA), and others are available. NTIS publishes a comprehensive semi-monthly abstract journal, *Government Reports Announcements* (GRA), listing the 60,000 reports it receives each year. A companion journal, *Government Reports Index* (GRI), has five separate indexes: subject, personal author, corporate author, report number, and contract number. An annual index is also published. NTIS also publishes easy-to-scan, weekly subject-oriented abstracts bulletins—"Weekly Government Abstracts." One title in this new series is *Environment Pollution and Control*, available for annual subscription. It includes abstracts of all Environmental Impact Statements.

"NTISearch," an NTIS service, provides a comprehensive search of the total NTIS collection in answer to specific questions. It employs an on-line computer search system and results in printed lists of document abstracts pertinent to the question. Searches are based on keywords assigned to all documents entering the system. A typical document is indexed by 12 terms, which gives NTISearch a retrieval capability far surpassing that of the printed NTIS Indexes. You may contact NTIS: c/o U.S. Dept. of Commerce, Rm. 1098, 14th & E Sts., N.W., Washington, D.C. 20230.[7]

The Federal Documents Section and the Science and Technology Division of the Library of Congress provide reference services and may be of assistance in locating documents through the use of their card catalogs. The Photoduplication Service may under certain conditions make available for research use copies of nonrestricted materials in the Library's collections—this is in lieu of loan of the materials, or in place of manual transcriptions.

The National Library of Medicine (NLM), Bethesda, Maryland, collects information materials exhaustively in some 40 biomedical areas, and to a lesser degree, in many related subject fields. Its computer-produced *Index Medicus* is a comprehensive subject-author index to articles from approximately 2200 world-wide journals. To provide rapid dissemination of the information, this Library has been developing a network arrangement through which interlibrary loan services can be shared more efficiently in the United States. NLM's Toxicology Information Program publishes the quarterly *Toxicity Bibliography*; it also compiles a toxicology vocabulary and maintains a roster of expert advisers. For information about NLM services, write: Office of Public Information, National Library of Medicine, 8600 Rockville Pike, Bethesda, MD 20014.

The National Agricultural Library (NAL) has more than 2 million volumes, including literature in 50 languages from 200 foreign countries. NAL publishes indexes and bibliographies in its subject fields; provides data to produce the *Bibliography of Agriculture*, a monthly index to the world's literature on agriculture and related chemical and biological subjects; and has reference services, including the copying (with a service charge) of materials in its collection.

However, NAL does not distribute the U.S. Department of Agriculture publications. They are available for purchase from: Office of Information, Administration Building, Room 502, U.S. Department of Agriculture, Washington, D.C. 20250.

Many other federal departments and agencies have their own libraries or information centers and sell their publications. A few of interest include:

U.S. Department of Interior, Natural Resources Library, 19th and C Streets, N.W., Washington, D. C. 20240

National Oceanic and Atmospheric Administration, Atmospheric Sciences Library, 8060 13th Street, Silver Springs, Maryland 20910

National Oceanic and Atmospheric Administration, Marine and Earth Sciences Library, 6001 Executive Boulevard, Rockville, Maryland 20852

Bureau of Mines, Department of Interior, Washington, D.C. 20240

Environmental Protection Agency, 401 M Street, N.W., Washington, D.C. 20460

U.S. Geological Survey, Department of Interior, National Center, Reston, Virginia 23092

A 1970 publication sponsored by the Office of Education, entitled *A Study of Resources and Major Subject Holdings Available in U.S. Federal Libraries Maintaining Extensive or Unique Collections of Research Materials*, may also be of help. This document is available for purchase as ED 043350 from: ERIC Document Reproduction Service, Oryx Press, 2214 N. Central Avenue, Phoenix, AZ 85004. More than 3,600,000 U.S. patents have been issued for mechanical, electrical, and chemical inventions. The weekly *Official Gazette of the United States Patent Office* contains an abstract and key drawing for each patent granted during the week, and also has helpful indexes. Printed copies of any patent may be purchased from the Patent Office, Washington, D.C. The complete specification and drawings of all newly issued U.S. patents are also available on 16mm microfilm from NTIS. This service is furnished by subscription only. NTIS also announces Government-owned patents and patent applications that are available for licensing in its *Weekly Government Abstracts* series, and in *Government Reports Topical Announcements*.

Some governmental working papers, preliminary reports, minutes of meetings, and other internal documents may be obtained from the issuing agencies by following the procedures specified in the "Freedom of Information Act" (Public Information Section of the Procedure Act, June 1967). This act also defines when a document may be withheld from the public and requires that each agency publish in the Federal Register the office to be contacted and the procedures to be followed when requesting information. In 1970 a two-volume compilation of these procedures (*Legally Available U.S. Government Information as a Result of the Public Information Act*) was published by Output Systems Corporation, Arlington, VA 22202.

NOTES

1. This section has been heavily influenced by four works, which you may wish to study for greater detail: (1) Beveridge, W.I.B., 1957, *The art of scientific investigation,* 3rd ed., New York, Vintage Books, pp. 3–18. (2) Lasworth, E. J., 1972, *Reference sources in science and technology,* Metuchen, Scarecrow Press, pp. ix–xiv, 1–239. (3) Wilson, E. B., 1952, *An introduction to scientific research,* New York, McGraw-Hill Book Co., Inc., pp. 10–20. (4) Knox, W. T., 1972, *Document Services*; unpublished pre-print: Cincinnati, National Environmental Information Symposium, September 24–27, 1972.

2. Nathan Grier Parke suggested (1958, *Guide to the literature of mathematics and physics, including related works on engineering science,* 2nd rev. ed., New York, Dover Press): "There are eight important traits a library researcher should possess before attempting a systematic search." His list: imagination, mental flexibility, thoroughness, orderliness, persistency, observation, judgment, and accuracy.

3. The New York State Education Department's Division of Library Development in 1976 published *Procedures for processing requests for computerized literature searches.* That document includes general and applied information about computerized literature searches. In theory, a computerized literature search is suitably carried out when a question may be posed in Boolean logic. One might (symbolically) ask the computer: "find all citations to literature in your memory that include topics A & B, but not C." From page 6 of the New York State report: " . . . As an example of this process, posit that a researcher is interested in the use of lithium to treat schizophrenia. When lithium is searched as a single term there are 1200 citations in the data

base, and schizophrenia, searched as a single term, produces 2500 citations. When the two terms are connected by the Boolean logical operator 'AND' the computer retrieves 43 citations. . . ." This efficient search can be accomplished in seconds or minutes.

4. One reviewer has suggested you'd be interested to look up "strange" and "charm" in a general dictionary and in a physics dictionary. It is easy to think of others that are defined differently.

5. Individuals have open access to many large data bases. Persons or organizations having personal microcomputers can, for a small fee, subscribe to services that take advantage of the easy transmissibility of selected bits of information from larger data bases. For example, in addition to computational, accounting, editing, and data-storage functions, owning or renting such a home or office unit gives you access to wire services' news reports, airplane reservations, selected (by subject or section) newspaper information (e.g., reviews of plays, obituaries), Dow Jones values and other stock market analyses and listings.

6. *DAI* was in the past called *Dissertation Abstracts* and *Microfilm Abstracts*.

7. Agency addresses change from time to time. This address, and others listed in this chapter, should be verified.

INDEXES | ABSTRACTS | RESEARCH PAPERS

INTRODUCTION

The preceding chapter outlined or detailed the kinds of literature resources that were available to begin or support literature searches. **This chapter goes further, citing important examples of those various kinds of literature resources. It will help you locate specific starting points for many literature searches, and will test your abilities in tracking down particular bits of information from the literature.** After completing the exercises that conclude this chapter, you should be able to use appropriate literature sources to acquire virtually any scientific information.

During the course of your work or studies, you may find valuable sources that are not listed here. Add these to the references cited in the various general source lists below (beginning on p. 72). Later you'll probably be glad to refer back to them; this can save you many hours when you make another literature search.

Don't attempt to memorize source lists, but do learn what these resources contain and where the works listed can be found. Getting to know them comes with using them for the searches at the end of this chapter and in your own research.

GENERAL SOURCE LISTS

Findings from a study of migraine patients made by an Englishman were published in 1968. Do you know how to find where they were published? Can you determine the Englishman's name? To be able to answer picayune questions of this sort should be your goal as you work your way through this chapter. (You should also be able to correctly answer those questions.)

Recognizing that learning to use the literature is like learning laboratory techniques, you'll quickly discover that there is no substitute for "hands-on experience." So: go to the library. There study the format of representative books from the lists that follow this section; determine the kinds of materials each covers, and the manner in which it is presented. As these listings only sample various types of reference materials available in several disciplines, it should be clear that the lists are not intended to comprise a definitive bibliography of reference materials.

For convenience we have included with each reference the Card Catalog numbers assigned to it in a representative library that uses the Library of Congress classification system. Please note that the citations for works on the several pages that follow are incomplete. They do not follow the form recommended for use in the formal bibliographies you will compile (p. 152). Most are reference books and can be located quickly among your library's collections. In some instances you may find other editions or similar works that will serve you as well as those listed here. Your time is better spent using what's on hand than in trying to track down all the works listed.

DICTIONARIES AND GLOSSARIES

Abbreviations Dictionary. 6th ed. Desola, Ralph. Elsevier North-Holland, 1981. PE1693.D4 1981

Acronyms and Initialism Dictionary. 6th ed. Gale, 1978. P365.G3 1978

Chambers Dictionary of Science and Technology. Barnes & Noble, 1972. Q123.D53 1972

Chemical Synonyms and Trade Names. 8th ed. Gardner, William, and Cooke, Edward I. International Publications Service, 1978. TP9.G28 1978

Cyclopedic Medical Dictionary. 13th ed. Taber, Clarence W., F. A. Davis, 1977. R121.T18 1977

Dictionary of Economic Plants. 2nd ed. Uphof, J. C. Lubrecht & Cramer, 1968. QK9.U6 1968

Dictionary of Geology. 5th ed. Challinor, John, ed. Oxford University Press & Wales University Press, 1978. QE5.C45

Dictionary of Named Effects and Laws in Chemistry, Physics and Mathematics. 4th ed. Ballentyne, D. W., and Lovett, D. R. Chapman and Hall, 1980. Q123.B3 1980

Dictionary of Nutrition and Food Technology. 3rd ed. Bender, Arnold E. Chemical Publishing Co., 1976. TX349.B4 1976

Dictionary of the Biological Sciences. Gray, Peter. Van Nostrand Reinhold, 1967. QH13.G68

Dictionary of the Environment. Allaby, Michael. Van Nostrand Reinhold, 1977. QH540.4 A44 1977

Dictionary of Zoology. 3rd ed. Leftwich, A. W. Constable, 1973. QL9.L4 1973

Dorland's Illustrated Medical Dictionary. 25th ed. Dorland, William B. Saunders, 1974. R121.D73 1974

Fairchild's Dictionary of Textiles. 6th ed. Wingate, Isabel B. Fairchild Publications, 1979. TS1309.F1 1979

French-English Science and Technology Dictionary. 4th ed. DeVries, Louis. McGraw-Hill, 1976. Q123.D37 1976

German-English Science Dictionary. 4th ed. DeVries, Louis. McGraw-Hill, 1978. Q123.D4 1978

Glossary of Geology. 2nd ed. Bates, Robert L., and Jackson, Julie, eds. American Geological Institute, 1980. QE5.G37 1980

Glossary of Mineral Species. Fleischer, Michael. Mineralogical Record, Inc., 1975. QE357.F54 1975

Henderson's Dictionary of Biological Terms. 9th ed. Holmes, Sandra, ed. Van Nostrand Reinhold, 1979. QH13.H38 1979

Illustrated Dictionary of Eponymic Syndromes and Diseases and Their Synonyms. Jablonsky, Stanley. William B. Saunders, 1969. R121.J24

McGraw-Hill Dictionary of Scientific & Technical Terms. 2nd ed. Lapedes, Daniel N., ed. McGraw-Hill, 1978. Q123.M15 1978

Mathematics Dictionary. 4th ed. James, Glenn, and James, Robert C. Van Nostrand Reinhold, 1976. QA5.J32 1976

Naming the Living World. Savory, T. H. Wiley, 1962. QH33.S3

Russian-English Scientific and Technical Dictionary. Alford, M. H., and Alford, V. L. Pergamon, 1970. Q123.A4

Sourcebook of Biological Names and Terms. 3rd ed. Jaeger, E. C. Thomas, 1978.

Stedman's Medical Dictionary. 22nd ed. Williams and Wilkins, 1972. R121.S8 1972

Webster's New Geographical Dictionary. G & C Merriam Co., 1977. G103.W45 1977

ENCYCLOPEDIAS

Dictionary of Organic Compounds. 4th ed. Oxford University Press, 1965 (& suppl., 1966–   ). QD251.D49 1965

Encyclopedia of Animal Care. 12th ed. West, Geoffrey P. Williams & Wilkins, 1977. SF609.M5 1977

Encyclopedia of Chemical Technology. 3rd ed. Kirk, R. E., and Othmer, D. F., eds. Wiley-Interscience, 1978–   . TP9.E685

Encyclopedia of Chemistry. 3rd ed. Hampel, Clifford A., and Hawley, Gessner G. Van Nostrand Reinhold, 1973. QD5.E58 1973

Encyclopedia of Computer Science. 2nd ed. Ralston, Anthony, ed. Van Nostrand Reinhold, 1978. QA76.E48 1978

Encyclopedia of Earth Science. Fairbridge, Rhodes W., ed. Dowden, Hutchinson & Ross, 1966–   .
v.I *The Encyclopedia of Oceanography*. 1966. GC9.F3

v.II *The Encyclopedia of Atmospheric Sciences and Astrogeology.* 1967. QC854.F34

v.III *The Encyclopedia of Geomorphology.* 1968. GB10.F3

v.IVA *The Encyclopedia of Geochemistry and Environmental Sciences.* 1972. QE515.F24

v.VI *The Encyclopedia of Sedimentology.* 1978. QE471.E49

v.VII *The Encyclopedia of Paleontology.* 1979. QE703.E52

v.VIII *The Encyclopedia of World Regional Geology, Part 1: Western Hemisphere.* 1975– . QE5.F33

v.XII *The Encyclopedia of Soil Science, Part 1: Physics, Chemistry, Biology, Fertility, and Technology.* 1979– . S592.E52

Encyclopedia of Microscopic Stains. Gurr, Edward. Williams and Wilkins, 1960. QH237.G87

Encyclopedia of Microscopy and Microtechnique. Gray, Peter, ed. Van Nostrand Reinhold, 1973. QH203.G8

Encyclopedia of Psychology. 2nd ed. Eysenck, H. J., ed. Seabury, 1979. BF31.E52 1979

Encyclopedia of the Biological Sciences. 2nd ed. Gray, Peter, ed. Van Nostrand Reinhold, 1970. QH13.G7 1970

Encyclopedic Dictionary of Mathematics. Nibon, Sugakki. MIT Press, 1977. QA5.N5 1977

Encyclopedic Dictionary of Physics. Pergamon, 1961– . QC5.E52

International Geographic Encyclopedia and Atlas. Houghton-Mifflin, 1979. G105.I57

McGraw-Hill Encyclopedia of Environmental Science. Lapedes, Daniel N. McGraw-Hill, 1974. QH540.4.M3

McGraw-Hill Encyclopedia of Science and Technology. 5th ed. McGraw-Hill, 1982. Q121.M3 1982

The Merck Index: An Encyclopedia of Chemicals and Drugs. 9th ed. Windholz, Martha, ed. Merck, 1976. RS51.M4 1976

Van Nostrand's Scientific Encyclopedia. 6th ed. Van Nostrand Reinhold, 1982. Q121.V3 1982

Water Encyclopedia. Todd, D. K., ed. Water Information Center, 1970. TD351.T63

YEARBOOKS AND REVIEW VOLUMES

Advances in Advanced Microbiology. Academic Press, 1958– QR1.A38

Advances in Ecological Research. Academic Press, 1963– QH540.A23

Annual Review of Astronomy and Astrophysics. Annual Reviews, 1963– QB1.A2884

Annual Review of Biochemistry. Annual Reviews, 1932—
QP501.A7

Annual Review of Ecology and Systematics. Annual Reviews,
1970—   QH540.A53

Annual Review of Physiology. Annual Reviews, 1939—
QP1.A535

Current Topics in Microbiology and Immunology. Springer-Verlag,
1914—   QR1.E6

McGraw-Hill Yearbook of Science and Technology. McGraw-Hill,
1962—   Q1.M13

Minerals Yearbook. U.S. Bureau of Mines, G.P.O., 1933—
I28.37:—

Progress in Thin-Layer Chromatography and Related Methods.
Humphrey Science, 1970—   . QD117.C5P7

Residue Reviews. Springer-Verlag, 1962—   . TX501.R47

Progress in Biophysics and Molecular Biology. Pergamon, 1950—
QH505.A1P76

Statistical Abstract of the United States. U.S. Department of Commerce, 1878—   . HA202.U6

Yearbook of Agriculture. U.S. Department of Agriculture, 1894—
S21.A35

HISTORIES

Discovery of the Elements. 7th ed. Weeks, M. E. Journal of Chemical
Education, 1968. QD466.W4 1968

History of Science. Taton, R. Basic Books, 1963—1966. Q125.T233

Introduction to the History of Science, 3 vols. in 5. Sarton, G. Williams
and Wilkins, 1927—1948. Q125.S32

*A Medical Bibliography: An Annotated Checklist of Texts Illustrating
the History of Medicine (Garrison & Morton).* 3rd ed. Morton,
L. T. Lippincott, 1970. Z6658.G243 1970

Short History of Scientific Ideas to 1900. Singer, C. J. Oxford University Press, 1959. Q125.S583

Source Book in Chemistry, 1400—1900. Leicester, H. M., and Klick-
stein, H. S. Harvard University Press, 1963. QD3.L47 1963

Source Book in Chemistry, 1900—1950. Leicester, H. M., ed. Harvard
University Press, 1968. QD11.L526 1968

Source Book in Geology, 1400—1900. Mather, K. F., and Mason, S. L.
Harvard University Press, 1967. QE3.M38

Source Book in Geology, 1900—1950. Mather, K. F., ed. Harvard
University Press, 1967. QE3.M38 1967

Source Book in Physics. Magie, William F. Harvard University Press,
1963. QC3.M26 1963

BIOGRAPHIES

Current

American Men and Women of Science. 14th ed. R. R. Bowker, 1979. Q141.A47

Current Biography Yearbook. H. W. Wilson, 1940–   . CT100.C8

International Who's Who. Europa, 1935–   . CT120.I5

Who's Who in America. Marquis, 1899–   . E663.W56

Who's Who of American Women. Marquis, 1958–   . CT3260.W5

Who's Who in Science in Europe. 3rd ed. Hodgson, 1978. Q145.W52 1978

Deceased

Biographical Memoirs. National Academy of Sciences (U.S.), 1877–   . Q141.N2

Dictionary of Scientific Biography. Scribner, 1970–   . Q141.D5

Dictionary of American Biography (DAB). American Council of Learned Societies. Scribner, 1943–   . E176.D562

Dictionary of National Biography (DNB). Oxford University Press, 1885–   . DA28.D4

National Cyclopedia of American Biography. James T. White, 1891–   . E176.N28

New York Times Index (under Obituaries). New York Times, 1851–   . AI21.N44

Persons of All Times

Biography Index. H. W. Wilson, 1946–   . Z5301.B5

Webster's Biographical Dictionary. G. & C. Merriam, 1980. CT1Q3.W4 1980

World Who's Who in Science. 1st ed. Marquis, 1968. Q141.W7

DIRECTORIES AND RESEARCH INFORMATION SOURCES

The AHA Guide to the Health Care Field. American Hospital Association, 1945–   . RA960.G8

American Library Directory. R. R. Bowker, 1923–   . Z731.A53

American Medical Directory. American Medical Association, 1906–   . R712.A1A6

Consumer Protection Directory. 2nd ed. Marquis, 1975. HC110.C63C65

Directory of Graduate Research. American Chemical Society, 1977. Z5525.U5A6 1977

Directory of Medical Specialists. 19th ed. Marquis, 1979. R712.A1D5 1979

Directory of Published Proceedings. InterDok, 1965–   . (quarterly) Z7403.D596

Directory of Scientific Directories. 3rd ed. Burkett, J., comp. Hodgson, 1979. Z7405.D55H47 1979

Directory of Special Libraries and Information Centers. 5th ed. Young, Margaret L. Gale, 1979. Z731.Y68 1979

Encyclopedia of Associations. 14th ed. Gale, 1980. HS17.G334

The Foundation Directory. 7th ed. Lewis, M. O. Foundation Center, 1979. AS911.F771 1979

Guide to American Directories. 10th ed. Klein, Bernard, ed. B. Klein Publications, 1978. Z5771.G8 1978

Indexers on Indexing. Harrod, Leonard Montague, ed. R. R. Bowker, 1978. Z695.9I52

Industrial Research Laboratories of the United States. 15th ed. Bowker, 1977. T176.I42 1977

Into Print. Hill, Mary, and Cochran, Wendell. William Kaufmann, Inc., 1977.

Official Museum Directory, 1978–79. American Association of Museums, National Register, 1978. AM10.A204 1978–1979.

Research Centers Directory. 6th ed. Palmer, Archie. Gale, 1979. Q145.R43 1979

Scientific Meetings. Scientific Meetings Publications, 1957–   . (quarterly). Q101.S63

Thomas Register of American Manufacturers. Thomas, 1906–   . T12.T63

World Meetings: Outside United States and Canada. World Meetings Information Center, 1968–   . (quarterly) Q101.W65

World Meetings: United States and Canada. World Meetings Information Center, 1963–   . (quarterly) Q11.T2

Yearbook of International Organizations. Union of International Associations, 1948–   . JX1904.A42

HANDBOOKS AND MANUALS

American Ephemeris and Nautical Almanac. U.S. Nautical Almanac Office. U.S. Government Printing Office, 1855–   . (annual) QB8.U1

American Institute of Physics Handbook. 3rd ed. Gray, Dwight E. American Institute of Physics, 1972. QC61.A5 1972

The Asphalt Handbook. Asphalt Institute, 1970. TN853.A7

Atlas of Electron Microscopy of Clay Minerals and their Admixtures. Beutelspacher, H. and Van der Marel, H. W. Elsevier, 1967. TP811.B4

Bergey's Manual of Determinative Bacteriology. 8th ed. Buchanan, R. E., ed. Williams and Wilkins, 1974. QR81.A5 1974

Index Bergeyana. Williams and Wilkins, 1966. (Companion volume to Bergey's Manual of Determinative Bacteriology). QR81.I5.

Biological Handbook Series. Altman, P. B., and Dittmer, D., eds. Federation of American Societies for Experimental Biology.
Biology Data Book. 2nd ed. 1972–1974. QH310.A392
Blood and Other Body Fluids. 1961. QP91.A515
Environmental Biology. 1966. QH310.A395
Growth. 1962. QH310.A4
Metabolism. 1968. QP141.A63
Respiration and Circulation. 1971. QP101.R47

Chemical Formulary. Bennett, H. Chemical Publishing Co., 1933– . TP141.B35

Clinical Toxicology of Commercial Products. 4th ed. Gosselin, R. E., et al. Williams and Wilkins, 1976. RA1211.G5 1976

Computer Dictionary and Handbook. 3rd ed. Sippl, C. J., and Sippl, R. J. Sams, 1980. QA76.15.S512

Dangerous Properties of Industrial Materials. 5th ed. Sax, N. I. Van Nostrand Reinhold, 1979. TS55.53 1979

Engineering Manual. Perry, Robert H. McGraw-Hill, 1976. TA151.P645 1976

Environment Reporter. Bureau of National Affairs, 1970– (loose-leaf). KF3775.A7E49

Environmental Information Sources Handbook. Wolff, G. R. ed. Simon & Schuster, 1974. GF503.W64

Fieldbook of Natural History. 2nd ed. Palmer, E. L. McGraw-Hill, 1975. QH45.2.P34 1975

Field Geology. 6th ed. Lahee, F. H. McGraw-Hill, 1961. QE28.L2 1961

Gray's Anatomy. 35th British ed. Warwick, R., and Williams, P. L., William B. Saunders, 1973. QM23.2.G73 1973a

Gray's Manual of Botany. 8th ed. Fernald, M. L. Van Nostrand Reinhold, 1970. QK117.G75

Lange's Handbook of Chemistry. 12th ed. Lange, Norbert A. McGraw-Hill, 1979. QD65.L36 1979

Handbook of Chemistry and Physics. Chemical Rubber Co., 1913– QD65.H3

Handbook of Environmental Control. Bond, R. G., and Straub, C. P., eds. Chemical Rubber Co., 1972–1978. TD145.C2

Handbook of Geochemistry. Wedepohl, Karl, H. Springer, 1969–. (loose-leaf) QE515.W42

Handbook of Laboratory Safety. 2nd ed. Steere, N. V., ed. Chemical Rubber Co., 1971. QD51.S88

Handbook of Microbiology. 2nd ed. Laskin, A. I., and Lechevalier, H. A. Chemical Rubber Co., 1977–1981. QR6.C2 1977

Handbook of Physical Constants. rev. ed. Clark, Sidney P., ed. Geological Society of America (Memoir 97), 1966.

An Introduction to the Rock-Forming Minerals. Deer, W. A., Howie, R. A., and Zussman, J. Wiley, 1966.

The Lippincott Manual of Nursing Practice. 2nd ed. Brunner, L. S., and Suddarth, D. S. Lippincott, 1978. RT52.B78 1978

Manual of Mineralogy after J. D. Dana. 19th ed. Hurlbut, C. S., and Klein, C. Wiley, 1977. QE372.D2 1977

Materials Handbook. 10th ed. Brady, G. S. McGraw-Hill, 1971. TA403.B75

Mathematical Handbook for Scientists and Engineers. 2nd. rev. ed. Korn, G. A. McGraw-Hill, 1968. QA40.K598 1968

Merck Manual of Diagnosis and Therapy. 13th ed. Berkow, R., ed. Merck, 1977. RC55.M4 1977

The New Britton and Brown Illustrated Flora of Northeastern United States and Adjacent Canada. Gleason, Henry A. Hafner, 1968. QK117.G5 1968

The Peterson Field Guide Series. Houghton-Mifflin, 1947–

A Field Guide to Animal Tracks. 2nd ed. Murie, Olaus, 1975. SK282.M8 1975

A Field Guide to Birds' Nests Found East of the Mississippi River. Harrison, Hal., 1975. QL675.H36

A Field Guide to Edible Wild Plants of Eastern and Central North America. Peterson, Lee, 1978. QK98.5U6P47

A Field Guide to Mexican Birds. Peterson, Roger Tory, and Chalif, Edward L., 1973. QL686.P47

A Field Guide to Pacific Coast Shells. rev. ed. Morris, Percy A., 1966. QL417.M72 1966

A Field Guide to Pacific States Wildflowers. Niehaus, T. F., 1976. QK143.N5

A Field Guide to Reptiles and Amphibians of Eastern and Central North America. 2nd ed. Conant, Roger, 1975. QL651.C65 1975

A Field Guide to Rocks and Minerals. 4th ed. Pough, Frederick H., 1976. QE367.P6 1976

A Field Guide to Rocky Mountain Wildflowers. Craighead, J. J., Craighead, F. C., and Davis, R. J., 1963. QK139.C9

A Field Guide to the Atlantic Seashore. Gosner, Kenneth L., 1979. QH95.7.G67 1979

A Field Guide to the Birds. 4th ed. Peterson, Roger Tory, 1980. QL681.P45 1980

A Field Guide to the Birds of Britain and Europe. 3rd ed. Peterson, R. T., Mountfort, G., and Hollom, P., 1974. QL690.A1P4 1974

A Field Guide to the Birds of Texas and Adjacent States. Peterson, Roger Tory, 1963. QL684.T494

A Field Guide to the Butterflies. Klots, Alexander B., 1951. QL548.K55

A Field Guide to the Ferns and Their Related Families. Cobb, B., 1956. QK525.C75

A Field Guide to the Insects of America North of Mexico. Borror, D. J., and White, Richard E., 1970. QL464.B65

A Field Guide to the Mammals. 3rd ed. Burt, William, 1976. QL715.B8 1976

A Field Guide to the Mammals of Britain and Europe. van den Brink, F. H., 1968. QL726.B6713 1968

A Field Guide to the Shells of our Atlantic and Gulf Coasts. 3rd ed. Morris, Percy A., 1973. QL416.M6 1973

A Field Guide to the Stars and Planets. Menzel, Donald, 1964. QB64.M4

A Field Guide to Trees and Shrubs. 2nd ed. Petrides, George, 1972. QK482.P43 1972

A Field Guide to Western Birds. 2nd ed. Peterson, Roger Tory, 1961. QL683.W4P4 1961

A Field Guide to Western Birds' Nests. Harrison, Hal., 1979. QL675.H38

A Field Guide to Western Reptiles and Amphibians. Stebbins, Robert C., 1966. QL651.S783

A Field Guide to Wildflowers of Northeastern and North-Central North America. Peterson, Roger Tory, and McKenney, Margaret, 1968. QK118.P5

Pharmacopoeia of the United States of America. (USPXX) 20th ed. United States Pharmacopeial Convention, 1979. RS141.2.P5 1979

Physicians Desk Reference. 34th ed. Medical Economics Co., 1980. RS75.P5 1980

Toxic Substances Sourcebook. Environment Information Center, 1978. T55.3.H3T69

Treatise on Invertebrate Paleontology. 2nd ed. Teichert, Curt, ed. Geological Society of America, 1970– . QE770.T72

The X-Ray Identification and Crystal Structure of Clay Minerals. Brown, G., ed. Mineralogical Society (of London), 1972. QE471.3.B85 1972

TABLES

Barlow's Tables of Squares, Cubes, Square Roots . . . 4th ed. Cromie, L. J. Chemical Publishing, 1960. QA47.B4 1960

Handbook of Mathematical Tables and Formulas. 5th ed. McGraw-Hill, 1973. QA47.B8 1972

Handbook of Mathematical Sciences. 5th ed. Beyer, William H. Chemical Rubber Co., 1978. QA47.H324 1978

Tables of Integrals, Series, and Products. Gradshetyn, I. S., *et al.* Academic, 1979. QA55.R993 1979

ATLASES AND GAZETTEERS

The Columbia Lippincott Gazetteer of the World. Seltzer, Leon, ed. Columbia University Press, 1962. G103.L7 1962

Commercial Atlas and Marketing Guide. Rand McNally, 1911– . (annual) HF1023.R18

Historical Atlas. 9th ed. rev. and updated. Shepherd, William R. Barnes & Noble, 1976. G1030.S4 1976

National Topographic Maps and Indexes. U.S. Geological Survey, 1944– . (microfiche) G3700.U5

New York Times Atlas of the World. Rev. ed. Times Books, 1981. G1019.N498 1981

The Times Atlas of the World. 5th ed. (comprehensive edition) Maps prepared by John Bartholomew & Son. Times Books, 1977. G1021.B3 1977

Webster's New Geographical Dictionary. rev. ed. G & C Merriam, 1977. G103.5.W42 1977

GUIDES TO THE LITERATURE

A Bibliography of Earth Science Bibliographies. Long, Harriet K. American Geological Institute, 1971. Z6031.L6 1971

Biological and Biomedical Resource Literature. Kerker, Ann E., and Murphy, Henry T. Purdue University, 1968. Z532.K7

A Brief Guide to Sources of Scientific and Technical Information. Herner, Saul. Information Resources, 1969. Q223.H42

Chemical Publications, Their Nature and Use. 4th ed. Mellon, M. G. McGraw-Hill, 1965. Z5521.M52 1965

The Geographical Digest. George Phillip & Son, Ltd., 1963. G1.G46

Geological Reference Sources. Ward, Dederick C., Wheeler, Marjorie W., and Pangborn, Jr., Mark W. Scarecrow Press, 1972.

Guide to Basic Information Sources in Chemistry. Anthony, Arthur. Halsted, 1979.

Guide to Basic Information Sources in Engineering. Mount, Ellis, ed. Halsted, 1976.

Guide to the Literature of Botany. Jackson, B. D. Hafner, 1964. (Reprint of 1881 ed.) Z5351.J12

Guide to the Literature of the Life Sciences. 8th ed. Smith, Roger C. Burgess, 1972. Z5320.S57 1972.

How to Find Out About Physics. Yates, B. Pergamon, 1965. Z7141.Y3 1965

How to Find Out in Chemistry. 2nd ed. Burman, C. R. Pergamon, 1966. Z5521.B9

How to Find Out in Mathematics. 2nd ed. Pemberton, J. E. Pergamon, 1970. Z6651.P4 1970

Literature of Chemical Technology. Smith, Julian, ed. American Chemical Society, 1968.

Medical Reference Works, 1679–1966. Blake, J. B., and Roos, C., eds. Medical Library Association, 1970–
———   ———, Suppl. I, 1967–1968.
———   ———, Suppl. II, 1969–1972.
———   ———, Suppl. III, 1973–1974.
Z675.M4 B636

Science and Engineering Sources. Malinowsky, H. R. Libraries Unlimited, 1967. Z7401.M28

Science and Technology. 3rd ed. Grogan, Davis J. Linnet Books, 1976. Q233.G7.6 1976

Searching the Chemical Literature. American Chemical Society, 1961. QD1.A355 #30

Science Reference Sources. Jenkins, Frances B. MIT Press, 1969. Z7401.J4 1969

Sources of Information Within the Social Sciences. 2nd ed. White,

Carl M. American Library Association, 1973. Z7161.W49

The ABS Guide to Recent Publications in the Social and Behavioral Sciences. American Behavioral Sciences, 1965. Z7161.A4

Using Books and Libraries. 3rd ed. Aldrich, Ella V., 1967.

Use of Biological Literature. 3rd ed. Bottle, R. T., ed. Butterworths, 1979. QD8.5.B6 1979

GENERAL BIBLIOGRAPHIES

American Bibliography (1639–1800). Evans, Charles. Publisher varies among the 14 vols., 1903–1959. (Reprint Peter Smith, 1941–1967) Z1215.E92

American Book Publishing Record (BPR). R. R. Bowker, 1960. (monthly) Z1201.A52

Books in Print (BIP), 2 vols. R. R. Bowker, 1948–   . (annual) Z1215.P972

Cumulative Book Index (CBI). H. W. Wilson, 1898–   . (monthly) Z1219.M78

Forthcoming Books. R. R. Bowker, 1966–   . (monthly) Z1219.P97

Guide to Reference Books. 9th ed. Sheehy, Eugene. American Library Association, 1976. Z1035.1.S43 1976

Guide to Reference Material. 3rd ed. Walford, A. J. Library Association, 1973–   . Z1035.W252

National Union Catalog, Pre-1956 Imprints. Mansell, 1968–1975. Z881.A1U518

———— ————, 1956–   . Rowman and Littlefield

Paperbound Books in Print. R. R. Bowker, 1955–   . (triannual) Z1033.P3P32

Publishers Trade List Annual. R. R. Bowker, 1873–   . (annual) Z1215.P972

Publishers Weekly. R. R. Bowker, 1872–   . Z1219.P98

Reference Books: A Brief Guide. 8th ed. Bell, Marion V., and Swidan, Eleanor A. Enoch Pratt Free Library, 1978. Z1215.P97

Subject Guide to Books in Print. R. R. Bowker, 1957. Z1215.P97

A World Bibliography of Bibliographies. Besterman, Theodore, ed. Rowman and Littlefield, 1963. Z1002.B56S4

SUBJECT BIBLIOGRAPHIES

(Examples, only, are given; add titles for your own areas of interest)

Bibliography of American History, 1769–1865. Hafner, 1967. (Reprint of work first published 1924–1929.) Z7408.U5M52

Catalogue of Scientific Papers, 1800–1900. Royal Society of London. Cambridge, 1914–1925. Z7403.R88

Guide to Gas Chromotography Literature. Signeur, Austin V. Plenum, 1964. Z5524.C55S5

Health Care Administration. Morris, D. A. Gale, 1978. Z6673.4.M66

History of the Life Sciences: An Annotated Bibliography. Smit, Pieter. Hafner, 1974. Z5320.S55

International Catalogue of Scientific Literature (1901–1914). International Council by the Royal Society of London, 1901–1919. Z7403.I61

Man and the Environment: A Bibliography of Selected Publications of the United Nations System 1946–1971. Winton, Harry N. M. Unipub, 1972. Z5322.E2W56

Publications of the Geological Survey. U.S. Geological Survey. U.S. Government Printing Office, 1879–1961. Then: *NEW PUBLI-CATIONS OF THE GEOLOGICAL SURVEY.* 1961–   . QE1.U5

Repertorium Commentationum . . . . Reuss, Jeremias D., 1801–1821. (Reprint Franklin, 1961) (publications of learned societies prior to 1800) Z5051.R44

LISTS OF PERIODICALS

Ayer Directory of Publications. Ayer Press, 1869–   . (annual) Z6951.A97

British Union Catalog of Periodicals (Incorporating World List of Scientific Periodicals). Butterworths, 1964–   . (quarterly) Z7403.W923

Catalogue of Scientific and Technical Periodicals, 1665–1895. 2nd ed. Bolton, Henry C. Smithsonian Institution, 1897. (1965 Johnson Reprint) Z7403.B69 1965

Catalogue of Scientific Serials of all Countries . . . , 1633–1876. Scudder, Samuel H. Harvard University Press, 1879. (1965 Kraus Reprint) Z7403.S46 1965

Irregular Serials and Annuals. R. R. Bowker 1967–   . Z6941.U522

Monthly Catalog of United States Government Publications. Superintendent of Documents, U.S. Government Printing Office, 1895–   . Z1223.A18 *(Serials Supplement)*

New Serial Titles. Library of Congress, 1950–1970. (monthly with quarterly and cumulative issues); and R. R. Bowker, 1971–   . Z6945.U5S42

Ulrich's International Periodical Directory, 1979–1980. 18th ed. R. R. Bowker, 1979. Z6941.U5

Union List of Serials in the Libraries of the United States and Canada.
3rd ed. H. W. Wilson, 1965. Z6945.U45 1965

*World List of Scientific Periodicals Published in the Years 1900–
1960.* 4th ed. 3v. Butterworths, 1963. Z7403.W923

*World List of Scientific Periodicals: New Periodicals Titles, 1960–
1968.* Butterworths, 1970. Z7403.W9

*World List of Scientific Periodicals: New Periodical Titles, 1969–
1972.* 4v. Butterworths, 1969–1972. (annual) Z7403.W9

INDEXING AND ABSTRACTING SERIALS

Abstracts in Anthropology. Greenwood, 1970–   . (quarterly)
GN1.A15

Abstracts of North American Geology. U.S. Geological Survey. U.S.
Government Printing Office, 1966–1971. QE75.A28

Applied Science and Technology Index. H. W. Wilson, 1913–   .
(monthly) Z7913.I7

Bibliography and Index of Geology. American Geological Institute,
1933–   . (monthly) Z6031.G4

Biological Abstracts (BA). BioSciences Information Service, 1926–   .
(semi-monthly) QH301.B37

Biological Abstracts/RRM. BioSciences Information Services,
1980–   .
(continues *Bioresearch Index*).

Biological and Agricultural Index. H. W. Wilson, 1916–   .
(monthly) Z5073.A46

Bioresearch Index. BioSciences Information Service, 1965–1979.
(monthly) Z5321.B672

Chemical Abstracts. Chemical Abstracts Service of the American
Chemical Society, 1907–   . (weekly) QD1.A51

Cumulative Index to Nursing and Allied Health Literature. Seventh-
Day Adventist Hospital Association. 1956–   . (bi-monthly)
Z6675.N7C8

Current Index to Journals in Education. National Institute of Education. Oryx Press, 1969–   . (monthly) Z5813.C8

Dissertation Abstracts International. University Microfilms,
1938–   . (monthly) Z5055.U5A53

Education Index. H. W. Wilson, 1929–   . (monthly) Z5813.E23

Energy Information Abstracts. Environment Information Center,
1976–   . TJ163.2.E482

Engineering Index. American Society of Mechanical Engineers, 1906– . (monthly) Z5851.E62

Environment Abstracts. Environment Information Center, 1971– . (monthly) GF1.E552

Environment Index. Environment Information Center, 1971– (annual) Z5322.E2E57

Environmental Periodicals Bibliography. Environmental Studies Institute, International Academy of Santa Barbara, 1972– . (bi-monthly) TD145.E59

Excerpta Medica. (44 sections). Excerpta Medica Foundation, 1971– . (monthly)

Government Reports Index. National Technical Information Service (NTIS). 1975– . (bi-weekly) Q158.5G67

Hospital Literature Index. American Hospital Association, 1955– . (quarterly) Z6675.H75.A51

Index Medicus. National Library of Medicine. U.S. Government Printing Office, 1960– . (monthly) Z6660.I422

Index to United States Government Periodicals. Infordata International, 1974– . Z1223.A915

International Nursing Index. American Journal of Nursing, 1966– . (quarterly) Z6675.N715

Mathematical Reviews. American Mathematical Society, 1940– . QA1.M76

Monthly Catalog, United States Government Publications. Superintendent of Documents, U.S. Government Printing Office, 1895– . (monthly) Z1223.A18

Pollution Abstracts. Oceanic Library and Information Center, 1970– . (bimonthly) TD172.P65

Psychological Abstracts. American Psychological Association, 1927– . (monthly) BF1.P65

Resources in Education (ERIC). U.S. Department of Health, Education, and Welfare. Educational Resources Information Center, 1966– . (monthly) Z5813.R4

Science Citation Index (SCI). Institute for Scientific Information, 1961– . (quarterly) Z7401.S365

Selected Water Resources Abstracts. Water Resources Scientific Information Center, U.S. Department of Interior, 1968– . (semi-monthly) TC1.S45

Technical Book Review Index. Special Libraries Association, 1935– . (monthly) Z7913.T36

United Nations Documents Index. United Nations, 1950– .
(monthly) JX1977.A2

Vertical File Index. H. W. Wilson, 1932– . (monthly)
Z1231.P2V48

MANUALS OF STYLE

CBE Style Manual. 4th ed. Style Manual Committee, Council of
Biology Editors. American Institute of Biological Sciences, 1978.
Z250.6.B5C6 1978

A Dictionary of Modern English Usage. Fowler, H. W. 2nd ed., rev. by
Sir Ernest Gowers. Oxford University Press, 1967. PE1628.F65
1967

Geowriting. 3rd ed. Cochran, W., Fenner, P., and Hill, M., eds.
American Geological Institute, 1979. QE48.85.C63 1979

Handbook for Scholars. van Leunen, Mary-Claire. Knopf, 1979.
PN146.V36 1979

A Manual for Writers of Term Papers, Theses, and Dissertations. 4th
ed. Turabian, Kate L., ed. University of Chicago, 1973.
LB2369.T8 1973

A Manual of Style. 12th ed., rev. University of Chicago, 1975.
Z253.C57 1975

A Style Guide for Chemists. Feiser, L. F., and Feiser, M. R. E.
Krieger, 1972 (c1960). QD7.F5 1972

Style Manual. rev. ed. U.S. Government Printing Office, 1973.
Z253.U58 1973

*Suggestions to Authors of the Reports of the United States Geological
Survey.* 6th ed. Bishop, Elna E., Eckel, Edwin B., and others, eds.
U.S. Government Printing Office, 1978.

INFORMATION SERVICES

Various information services are now offered commercially. The
nature, extent, and availability of these services are changing rapidly. Direct access by individuals is becoming easier and more common.
Your reference librarian can give you the most up-to-date information about services now available to you.

Remember that rates vary from one service to the next and
within services at different times of the day or week. For example,
THE SOURCE, a service that connects into many current data
sources (such as the daily Dow Jones index, newspaper sections, and
entertainment and travel ticketing facilities) charges from $2 to $15
per hour, depending upon whether it serves during a high- or low-
traffic time during the week.

Many of the larger libraries continue to maintain reference desk inquiry services—usually available through telephone inquiry. Their function is quite different from that of the sort described below.

ASCA (Automated Subject Citation Alert)

Institute for Scientific Information (ISI). A service of the publishers of *Science Citation Index* (*SCI*). ASCATOPICS is a weekly SCI report service that supplies listings of the latest and most important of the world's literature in 432 categories of the pure, applied, and social sciences.

BRS (Bibliographic Retrieval Services, Inc.)

BRS has grown out of the SUNY Biomedical Communication Network. These services were established in 1976 to provide low-cost on-line[1] access to a variety of major bibliographic data bases. Organized exclusively for on-line bibliographic retrieval.

DATRIX (Direct Access To Reference Information: A Xerox Service)

University Microfilms. DATRIX uses the same base from which *Dissertation Abstracts International* is produced. For any topic it can prepare a listing of relevant American and Canadian dissertations accepted between 1861 and the present.

DIALOG

Lockheed Information Systems. This information retrieval service provides interactive search access to many commercially available data bases. It is advertised as the "world's leading information system." It maintains a continuing program of research and development for information handling techniques. (See p. 59.)

GEO-REF

American Geological Institute. Provides access to the geological literature of the world and supplies a variety of services in information transfer. It is a current alerting service (it can flag certain data-base entries for subscribers) as well as an archival depository. Individual searches can be made on any combination of keyword entries desired, by on-line, multi-data-base tele-linkage.

IITRI

Illinois Institute of Technology Research Institute. Computer search center disseminates scientific information to industry, educational institutions, and research laboratories. Services include current awareness (flagging of requested items) and retrospective searches of the world's scientific literature made available by abstracting from organizational and professional society literature. Searches are customized for individual users.

MEDLINE (MEDical literature analysis and retrieval systems on-LINE)

National Library of Medicine. MEDLINE is a computerized on-line bibliographic searching system developed to provide rapid access to the literature of clinical and experimental medicine and allied health sciences.

National Referral Center, Science & Technology Division

Library of Congress. Provides a single place to which anyone with an interest in science and technology may turn for advice on where and how to obtain specific information on particular topics. The center does not provide technical details or bibliographic services, but refers requestors to those who can. It provides names, addresses, phone numbers, and brief descriptions of appropriate information resources.

NTIS (National Technical Information Service)

U.S. Department of Commerce. NTIS is the central vendor of reports on government-sponsored research, development, engineering, and analyses. SRIM (Selected Research in Microfiche) service sends the subscriber complete microfiche research reports only in subject areas selected by the subscriber.

SDC (Systems Development Corporation)

This is a multi-data-base on-line bibliographic search service. It provides interactive access from remote terminals for retrospective searches. Some of its data bases are: INFORM, a business management file by ABI (Abstracted Business Information, Inc.); CHEMCON, providing access to the American Chemical Society's comprehensive coverage; CAIN, the National Agriculture Library's Cataloging and Indexing System; ERIC, the educational data base developed and maintained by the U.S. Office of Education; MED-LINE (listed above); COMPENDEX, the computerized engineering indexes; and GEO-REF (listed above). Other scientific and technical data bases are added as they become available.

SSIE (Smithsonian Science Information Exchange)

Smithsonian Institution. SSIE is a clearinghouse for information on research in progress from all available sources. It helps bridge the critical information gap between the time a research project is initiated and the time its results are published. Its on-line service offers an immediate access for fast, cost-effective searching.

PRACTICE LITERATURE SEARCHES

Having studied the foregoing sections, you should now be ready to practice searching for information. A short review might be helpful before you begin.

Just as you develop your own laboratory techniques, so you will individualize your literature searching methodology. Generally speaking, your first step in the laboratory or library is "observation," whereby you collect all the information available on a particular subject. From that body of information you develop a tentative "hypothesis," which forms the basis for "experiments" to substantiate your "theories." If what you've posited is correct, you can formulate your "conclusion;" when your hypothesis doesn't stand up to experimentation, you'll have to try others until you determine the "truth." For the literature search, many data have already been gathered (the various lists that you've seen to this point), so you can begin by making sure that your search question is clearly defined. Analyze the question to discover what type of literature is likely to hold the answers you seek: will it be a book? a pamphlet? a government publication? a handbook? Will more than one reference be required? Several brief examples may help.

For the query, "How can I locate the address of the C. P. Rhoads Memorial Library of Sloan Kettering Institute for Cancer Research?" a directory would seem the most logical place to begin a search. On page (77) of this book you'll find listed the *Directory of Special Libraries and Information Centers*. Finding that work in your own library, then, you'll discover the information you seek. (If you have the 5th edition, 1979, entry #9210 on page 724 of *Volume I* will give you the correct address in Rye, New York.)

To find a periodical article, you'd look for appropriate periodical indexes and abstracts covering the subject area; a quick search by author or subject would tell you whether or not you've found an appropriate index.

When you need a dissertation, locate the abstract by author or subject in the *Comprehensive Dissertation Index* (discussed on p. 61–63 of this text). This leads you to the abstract in *Dissertation Abstracts International*, which gives you information on ordering a copy of the dissertation.

To "find a discussion of the relationship between air pollution and global climate," look at our list of encyclopedias (p. 74). Fairbridge's *Encyclopedia of Geochemistry and Environmental Science* would be an excellent source to check. You'd also likely look at your subject card catalog for more ideas.

To find a definition, go through our dictionaries and glossaries listing (p. 72). Available works cover almost every discipline.

Guides to the various disciplines should be used to assist you with areas whose resources are unfamiliar to you.

For the practice searches that follow, do one search at a time. First write down the type of source (primary, secondary, . . .) in which you think the information is likely to be contained. Formulate a search strategy and record the titles and call numbers of all the sources you think you should check. Use the sources listed in the first half of this chapter, and base your search strategy on chapter four's hints. Check the works you've selected, copying the appropriate page number (and other identifiers) once you believe you've found the correct reference. Only then consult the answer key provided on pages 122–123 to verify your answer. (Even the key doesn't locate the information by page number; you must actually consult the reference work.) The answer given in the key is one of several valid results. The key answer may be the best source; if yours is different, you can determine its validity simply by checking whether you can find there the information you seek.

Your task is to determine the *location* of the information in question. You need not record the information itself. Thus, in Search 1 the appropriate answer is a source title, not a number of liters.

In all cases, record the evaluation information as requested at the bottom of each page. It may reinforce your confidence in the process. The search exercises appear in order of increasing difficulty. (If you spend equal or less time on successive searches, then you are learning well.) The exercises give you an opportunity to put the theoretical aspects of a literature search to a practical test. As in a treasure hunt, you'll find some treasures easy to spot, while locating others may require a good bit of sleuthing. In the hunting process, you'll develop your own search technique and become more familiar with the practical aspects of your own library or learning center.

Work on actual practice searches until you feel you've mastered the search techniques that will enable you to answer any specific question; then go to the test searches (answers not given), which you should be able to complete with 100% accuracy. If you don't feel ready to attempt the evaluation searches after completing practice searches 1–20, try to find a reference librarian or someone else for counseling and, if necessary, additional practice searches.

Remember to reshelve the books you've used unless this is against the rules of your library.

Search 1: Where would you find out how much blood an average man
has?

Type of literature? _____

List books/journals checked   *Call No.*

Cite reference:

How long did it take you to complete this search? _____

How difficult was this search?
(Scale of 1−5 where 1=easy)_____

Search 2: A study was done on earthquakes and fluid pressure in the
Rangely oil field in Colorado. An article appeared about
1970, but the name of the researcher is not available. In
what journal did the article appear?

Type of literature? _____

   List books/journals checked   *Call No.*

Cite reference:

How long did it take you to complete this search? _____

How difficult was this search?
(Scale of 1–5 where 1=easy)_____

Search 3: A Swedish botanist by the name of Jimmy Persson has recently been studying Aegean flora and the genera of Cruciferae. The research was supposedly published in 1972. Where can this article be found?

Type of literature? _____

List books/journals checked   *Call No.*

Cite reference:

How long did it take you to complete this search? _____

How difficult was this search?
(Scale of 1–5 where 1=easy)_____

Search 4: In what source would you look to find where the English
periodical, *Nature*, is indexed?

Type of literature? _____

    List books/journals checked   *Call No.*

Cite reference:

How long did it take you to complete this search? _____

How difficult was this search?
(Scale of 1–5 where 1=easy)_____

Search 5: Where would you find a table of solution heats of various organic substances?

Type of literature? _____

List books/journals checked   *Call No.*

_____

Cite reference:

How long did it take you to complete this search? _____

How difficult was this search?
(Scale of 1−5 where 1=easy) _____

Search 6: Where would you look for an abstract of an article by J. A. Straczek on geochemical prospecting in India, written about 1960–1961?

Type of literature? _____

List books/journals checked	*Call No.*

Cite reference:

How long did it take you to complete this search? _____

How difficult was this search?
(Scale of 1–5 where 1=easy) _____

Search 7: Where would you find on what days there were eclipses of
the sun and moon in 1967?

Type of literature? _____

List books/journals checked   *Call No.*

Cite reference:

How long did it take you to complete this search? _____

How difficult was this search?
(Scale of 1–5 where 1=easy) _____

Search 8: Where would you find a definition of the term "tertiary" in
geology?

Type of literature? _____

    List books/journals checked   *Call No.*

Cite reference:

How long did it take you to complete this search? _____

How difficult was this search?
(Scale of 1–5 where 1=easy) _____

Search 9: Where can you find another name for dehydrite?

Type of literature? _____

    List books/journals checked   *Call No.*

Cite reference:

How long did it take you to complete this search? _____

How difficult was this search?
(Scale of 1−5 where 1=easy) _____

Search 10: Where can you find some biographical material and a
            bibliography of writings of Hugh St. Victor?

Type of literature? _____

List books/journals checked   *Call No.*

_____

Cite reference:

How long did it take you to complete this search? _____

How difficult was this search?
(Scale of 1–5 where 1=easy) _____

Search 11: Where would you find a reference to Parkinson's original
essay on the disease named for him?

Type of literature? _____

List books/journals checked   *Call No.*

Cite reference:

How long did it take you to complete this search? _____

How difficult was this search?
(Scale of 1–5 where 1=easy) _____

Search 12: Two University of Wisconsin chemists studied waste water thermal chemical pollution in Lake Michigan. An account of their study was published in 1972. What are the chemists' names?

Type of literature? _____

List books/journals checked   *Call No.*

Cite reference:

How long did it take you to complete this search? _____

How difficult was this search?
(Scale of 1−5 where 1=easy) _____

Search 13: An article appeared in *Nursing Clinics of North America* on a study that was done on six difficult patients. What is the name of the author and in what issue did it appear?

Type of literature? _____

    List books/journals checked   *Call No.*

Cite reference:

How long did it take you to complete this search? _____

How difficult was this search?
(Scale of 1−5 where 1=easy) _____

Search 14: The Battelle Memorial Institute of Columbus, Ohio, receives government subsidies and one of their reports was entitled "Final Three Years Progress on Study and Field Evaluation of Solar Sea Water Stills." The accession/report number is needed for ordering as well as the price. It came out about 1969.

Type of literature? _____

List books/journals checked   *Call No.*

Cite reference:

How long did it take you to complete this search? _____

How difficult was this search?
(Scale of 1−5 where 1=easy) _____

Search 15: How can you tell whether or not Eli Lilly & Co. of
        Indianapolis has a library?

Type of literature? _____

List books/journals checked   *Call No.*

Cite reference:

How long did it take you to complete this search? _____

How difficult was this search?
(Scale of 1−5 where 1=easy) _____

Search 16: One of us wrote a dissertation entitled, "Variations in Mineralogy and Trace Elements, Esopus Formation, Kingston, New York." When was it written? Where can you find an abstract?

Type of literature? _____

    List books/journals checked   *Call No.*

Cite reference:

How long did it take you to complete this search? _____

How difficult was this search?
(Scale of 1−5 where 1=easy) _____

Search 17: Find some data pertaining to the propagation and meta-
morphosis of insects.

Type of literature? _____

List books/journals checked   *Call No.*

Cite reference:

How long did it take you to complete this search? _____

How difficult was this search?
(Scale of 1–5 where 1=easy) _____

Search 18: Where can you find a recipe for a bath oil?

Type of literature? _____

    List books/journals checked   *Call No.*

Cite reference:

How long did it take you to complete this search? _____

How difficult was this search?
(Scale of 1−5 where 1=easy) _____

Search 19: An Englishman did a follow-up study of 92 patients who had migraine headaches and his findings were published in 1968. What was his name and where were they published?

Type of literature? _____

List books/journals checked   *Call No.*

Cite reference:

How long did it take you to complete this search? _____

How difficult was this search?
(Scale of 1−5 where 1=easy) _____

Search 20: James Joseph Gallagher presented a paper entitled "A Comparison of Individualized and Group Instruction in Science: Effects on Third Grade Pupils" at the Annual Meeting of the National Association for Research in Science Teaching held in Minneapolis in 1970. Where can a copy of this be secured?

Type of literature? _____

    List books/journals checked   *Call No.*

Cite reference:

How long did it take you to complete this search? _____

How difficult was this search?
(Scale of 1–5 where 1=easy) _____

TEST LITERATURE SEARCHES

If you feel confident after completing your practice searches (pp. 92–111), then you should be ready to proceed with these searches. The following ten searches will test your ability to track down information. Complete them exactly as you did the practice searches.

Search 21: A *National Estuary Study* was prepared by the Sport Fisheries and Wildlife Bureau of the U.S. Government. How many volumes are there in the departmental edition, and what are their prices?

Type of literature? _____

List books/journals checked   *Call No.*

Cite reference:

How long did it take you to complete this search? _____

How difficult was this search?
(Scale of 1–5 where 1=easy) _____

Search 22: Theodore W. Richards was awarded the Nobel Prize. Find
a discussion of his contributions to science, and a bibliography of some of his writings.

Type of literature? _____

List books/journals checked   *Call No.*

Cite reference:

How long did it take you to complete this search? _____

How difficult was this search?
(Scale of 1–5 where 1=easy) _____

Search 23: Find a discussion relating mineral particles and human
disease.

Type of literature? _____

List books/journals checked   *Call No.*

Cite reference:

How long did it take you to complete this search? _____

How difficult was this search?
(Scale of 1–5 where 1=easy) _____

Search 24: Carl Djerassi has written extensively in the field of organic chemistry. Find an extensive listing of his publications. At what institution was he teaching in 1971?

Type of literature? _____

List books/journals checked   *Call No.*

Cite reference:

How long did it take you to complete this search? _____

How difficult was this search?
(Scale of 1−5 where 1=easy) _____

Search 25: Locate a table of air pollutant emissions from transportation sources taken from an interstate air pollution study in 1963.

Type of literature? _____

List books/journals checked   *Call No.*

Cite reference:

How long did it take you to complete this search? _____

How difficult was this search?
(Scale of 1–5 where 1=easy) _____

Search 26: It has frequently been advocated that there should be a reduction or elimination of fish-eating birds in salmon waters. A study has been made in recent years on mergansers on northern Cape Breton Island. When and where did this article appear?

Type of literature? _____

List books/journals checked   *Call No.*

Cite reference:

How long did it take you to complete this search? _____

How difficult was this search?
(Scale of 1-5 where 1=easy) _____

Search 27: How many newspapers does Gaylord, Michigan, have? What are their names, and how often are they published? How large is Gaylord?

Type of literature? _____

List books/journals checked   *Call No.*

_____

Cite reference:

How long did it take you to complete this search? _____

How difficult was this search?
(Scale of 1–5 where 1=easy) _____

Search 28: Find a description of the drug Oreticyl. For what is it
used, and what are some of the adverse reactions a
patient could experience? Who is the manufacturer?

Type of literature? _____

List books/journals checked   *Call No.*

Cite reference:

How long did it take you to complete this search? _____

How difficult was this search?
(Scale of 1−5 where 1=easy) _____

Search 29: On 31 May 77, citing studies linking benzene to leuke-
mia, the Environmental Protection Agency listed the
chemical as a hazardous air pollutant, under the Clean
Air Act, and began to take steps to determine the extent
of control needed to curb emissions of the chemical.
Locate highlights of the statements made by Jacqueline
Warren and Eula Bingham about this development, and
locate the Clean Air Act. (2 references required)

Type of literature? _____

List books/journals checked   *Call No.*

Cite reference:

How long did it take you to complete this search? _____

How difficult was this search?
(Scale of 1−5 where 1=easy) _____

Search 30: Near the middle of this century, Mssrs. Arvin and Hunn
patented a process for producing alkylphenols. What
company did they represent, and what is the date and the
number of the patent? Where can you find the index to
Gigiyena I Sanitariya in order to determine whether an
article about their findings appeared in that periodical,
and if so, to be able to locate it? (2 references required)

Type of literature? _____

List books/journals checked   *Call No.*

Cite reference:

How long did it take you to complete this search? _____

How difficult was this search?
(Scale of 1–5 where 1=easy) _____

SEARCH REFERENCES

Reference for Search 1: (Secondary) Altman and Dittmare, *Biology Data Book.*

Reference for Search 2: (Secondary) *Abstracts of North American Geology,* 12/1970, under Colorado—earthquakes; C. Barry Raleigh, #01969.

Reference for Search 3: (Secondary) *Biological Abstracts,* vol. 53, June 1, 1972, #58939.

Reference for Search 4: (Tertiary) *Ulrich's International Periodical Directory.*

Reference for Search 5: (Secondary) *International Critical Tables,* vol. 5.

Reference for Search 6: (Secondary) *Chemical Abstracts* 1962, 57.

Reference for Search 7: (Secondary) *American Ephemeris and Nautical Almanac,* 1976.

Reference for Search 8: (Secondary) *Glossary of Geology;* p. 295, Challinor, *Dictionary of Geology.*

Reference for Search 9: (Secondary) *Chemical Synonyms and Trade Names.*

Reference for Search 10: (Secondary) *Dictionary of Scientific Biography,* vol. 6.

Reference for Search 11: (Secondary) Garrison and Marton's *Medical Bibliography.*

Reference for Search 12: (Secondary) *Chemical Abstracts,* vol. 78, #10, 1973, #61937t, Subject Index.

Reference for Search 13: (Secondary) *International Nursing Index,* 1971, under "Nursing Care", M. C. Parsons, *et al.,* or *Cumulative Index to Nursing Literature.*

Reference for Search 14: (Secondary) USGRDR, *Corporate Author Index,* vol. 69 (1969).

Reference for Search 15: (Tertiary) *Directory of Special Libraries and Information Centers.*

Reference for Search 16: (Secondary) *Dissertation Abstracts* Index, vol. 3, part 2; *Dissertation Abstracts,* vol. 24.

Reference for Search 17: (Secondary) Altman and Dittmare, *Biology Data Book.*

Reference for Search 18: (Secondary) Bennett, *Chemical Formulary,* vol. IV and vol. V.

Reference for Search 19: (Secondary) *Cumulated Index Medicus,* vol. 9, 1968, Subject Index H–O, under "Migraine."

Reference for Search 20: (Primary) *ERIC* 1970, ED 037361 (from ERIC microfiche).

NOTES

1. This means that questions are responded to on a while-you-wait basis. Batch processing is the usual electronic alternative, and involves saving questions to be posed to a computer until a batch is accumulated; those questions are processed at one time (often overnight), allowing computer efficiency. In the latter case, "connect time" may be very low, though per-unit-time costs may be high.

Understanding Data-Handling Procedures 6

INTRODUCTION

We live in an exciting era for data retrieval technology. New concepts and processes for storing and retrieving information are continually being developed and implemented. Information of all sorts is becoming more rapidly and less expensively available than ever before to all of us. Everyone involved in scientific investigation and research should know about retrieval systems already in operation, as well as those now under development. **This chapter will help you assess the strengths and weaknesses of the various systems and give you insight into the historical development, the present status, and some future prospects for data storage and retrieval methods and techniques.**

On completing this chapter, you should be able to describe the data-handling procedures in use today and the changes proposed through emerging technologies. Because changes are being introduced rapidly in some technologies, you might best be able to remain current on the topic by seeking out the latest advertising literature of data systems manufacturers. (The previous chapter should have taught you where these might be found.) Such material will acquaint you with commercial research and development in, as well as the cost of, data-handling systems.

This chapter emphasizes the hallmark of all effective information systems: good organization. Questions later in this chapter should help you to organize what you know about the nature of information and the various ways it can be transmitted and stored. One question asks you to apply what you've learned to an information-system need of your own.

In answering the questions that conclude this chapter you can let your imagination run free, for there are few "wrong" answers. This chapter is intended to stimulate contemplation and, where appropriate, discussion. It stands in contrast to earlier chapters, where questions have rather fixed bounds, and most require a specific answer or one of only a few good responses.

DATA BASES AND INFORMATION TRANSFER[1]

Primitive peoples lacked the cultural history and communicative coordination to develop a system of writing, substances upon which to write, instruments with which to write, and places to store the finished products—either for reference or posterity. Before they invented writing, early humans must have commemorated notable places or things by nonwritten visual symbols: rock cairns; knotted cords; bone beads; scratches on wood, rock, and (later) metals. Among early peoples who had language but not yet writing (as among primitive peoples today), accumulated knowledge survived by means of word-of-mouth transmittals of memorized information—either during daily activities or at special ceremonial occasions—to all members of younger generations for general information.[2]

Writing systems all developed from crude rock carvings of three types: (1) pictographs, which pictured objects; (2) ideographs, which represented ideas suggested by the objects; and, (3) phonographs, which represented the sound of an action or object. Such writing systems were probably later used on vegetable fibers, cloth, wood, skins, clay, and metal; only examples on clay, metal, and rock have survived.

INFORMATION TRANSFER DURING ANTIQUITY

The earliest known writing system, cuneiform writing, was developed by the Sumerian civilization that flourished in the Tigris-Euphrates Valley during the 4th and 3rd millenia B.C. Their written record, produced with wedge-shaped styli on wet clay tablets (later baked hard), dates back at least to 3100 B.C. These tablets form mankind's first preserved records of schools, social reforms, tax levies, and political, social, and philosophical thinking. Later Sumerian works on clay tablets and cylinders preserved mankind's oldest known literary efforts. Libraries were established. One at Tello has been found to contain 30,000 tablets.

After the sack of Ur by the Elamites in 2357 B.C., Sumeria's culture was absorbed and augmented by the Babylonian Empire in Lower Mesopotamia. Babylonian syllable characters gradually evolved from the Sumerian. Until Babylonia collapsed in 698 B.C., tablets were used to record matters of government, law, history and religion (e.g., Hamurabi's Code). Although there were probably many libraries, our present knowledge of these people comes primarily from copies of Babylonian writings made for Assurbanipal, King of Assyria.

The Nineveh Library of Assurbanipal (who died about 626 B.C.) contained tens of thousands of clay tablets, translated into Assyrian and copied by royal scribes according to subject or type. Assyrian characters are similar to the Babylonian. The Behistun Inscription (Persian, Babylonian, Elamitic) is the key to translation of many of the Nineveh documents.

Egyptian writings also date from about 3000 B.C. Hieroglyphics (literally, sacred carvings) were inscribed on monuments of wood or stone, or were written with reed points on papyrus sheets—the latter sometimes joined together to form scrolls. The Egyptians, who used hieroglyphs (combinations of some 700 characters) for sacred carvings until at least 395 A.D., also developed an alphabet of 24 consonants, which were mixed with pictographs, ideographs, and syllabic signs for use in secular manuscripts. Manuscripts were written in columns, without word spaces, punctuation marks, or titles. The well-known Rosetta Stone, with its parallel inscriptions in hieroglyphics, Egyptian demotic, and Greek writing, provided the clues that enabled the translation of the old Egyptian scripts. In libraries, the papyrus scrolls were kept in clay jars or metal cylinders with a key identifying word on the outside or end.

Other Semitic peoples living in the Fertile Crescent during and after the 3rd millenium B.C. included the Phoenicians, Aramaeans, and Hebrews. The Phoenicians, as the important traders of the time, were largely responsible for disseminating through the Middle East the use of papyrus and of a cursive alphabet (developed in Egypt, Crete, and Syria) that later formed the basis of Greek and all European writing. The Aramaeans, too, abandoned cuneiform and adopted an alphabet similar to that of the Phoenicians. Aramaic was the language spoken by Christ, and it was written in an alphabet essentially the same as that used by modern Arabs. Hebrew writing dates back at least to Moses and the Tablets of Law, but the old Canaanite script dates only to about 1200 B.C.[3]

Hebrews produced the works of the Old Testament, written on scrolls of papyrus, leather, and parchment, in an alphabet of 22 consonants similar to those of the Phoenicians, but in a language said to be "the purest and most complete of the Semitic family of languages" (Gates, 1962, p. 10). Religious and legal matters were inseparable, because the latter concerned the traditional interpretation of the former, and were the largest part of Hebrew writings, carefully preserved in the temples.

At least as early as the 3rd millenium B.C., the Chinese also were writing—on bone, shell, bamboo stalks, wooden tablets, silk, and linen, using quill styli or brushes to produce mainly ideographic characters.

Known Greek writings date only from about 776 B.C. In rough chronological order, Greek writings appeared on leaves or bark, stone or bronze (for inscriptions), and wax-coated wooden tablets (for messages or notes); later (6th century B.C.) on papyrus; and, during Hellenistic times, on parchment and vellum. (Of their literature from

before the 5th century B.C., when new forms of poetry were developing, only fragments have survived.) With the spreading influence of
Greece went a broadening of literary activities, including—especially after the death of Alexander (323 B.C.)—a new emphasis on
scientific knowledge, on art, and on rhetoric. Greek "books"—i.e.,
rolls, wax tablets, and codexes (sheets of parchment or papyrus fas-
tened together like the pages of today's books)—were produced in
large quantities during this, the Hellenistic Period. Gradually the
Greeks modified the Phoenician-style alphabet; they added vowels
and lower-case letters; by the end of the Hellenistic Period, punctuation had been introduced, and words were written across the page
from left to right. The Greeks signaled topic changes in written texts
by means of the *paragraphos*, a horizontal dividing line.

Libraries of various sorts were developed. The greatest in the
ancient world was probably that at Alexandria, having at the time of
the Roman conquest some 700,000 rolls in many languages. "As a
matter of general interest," wrote O. T. Hayward, in his 1971 *Dimensions of a Planet* (New York, McGraw-Hill, p. 8), "one of the principal
reasons the Alexandrian library had become so important was that
the sweet, little, old librarian [Demetrius, about 285 B.C.] . . . had not
only maintained a quiet reading room, he had also operated a small
overdue-book goon squad. . . . Travelers arriving in Alexandria were
met at the quayside by a batch of illiterate, armed, and hairy library
aides looking for overdue books. Any book they found in baggage or
on person was automatically overdue at the library in Alexandria. . . ." Works obtained by this method were copied; the originals
were then cataloged and shelved at Alexandria, and copies were later
given to the former owners "with no particular thanks. It was a
low-budget operation for a big library . . ." (Hayward, 1971, p. 8).

By the time they conquered Greece, the Romans had been heavily
influenced by Hellenistic culture—especially in matters pertaining
to literature, writing, and writing materials. Gradually the Romans
developed a non-cursive handwriting (i.e., letters not joined together)
for nonliterary use; by the 4th century A.D. they had evolved uncial
script, the large, rounded letters that were used for about four centu-
ries. The Roman roll was gradually superceded by the codex, which
was generally used for Christian works from the 2nd century A.D.
Pagan writings continued on papyrus for some time. For Roman
generals and patrician citizens, private libraries were status symbols
of a sort, and books were among the spoils of war. Public libraries,
open to all—slaves included—began to appear shortly before the
birth of Christ. Roman libraries, having lasted 500 years, were
destroyed during the barbarian invasions.

INFORMATION TRANSFER DURING THE MIDDLE AGES

Largely through monastic efforts, some literature survived the barbarian onslaughts of the Dark Ages (400–900 A.D.). Secular literature was transferred to Moslem libraries and monasteries in Constantinople, and many writings were preserved in Christian monasteries. Much of our knowledge of the ancient world comes from handwritten copies made by monks in countless scriptoria throughout the "civilized Western world"—books of the Bible, Homeric epics, Virgilian poetry, Greek dramas, and the scientific, legal, and philosophical works of the great minds of antiquity. Plain or dyed parchment or vellum, quill pens, and colored inks were the raw materials of the monastic rolls and codexes, which were often elaborately illuminated. The beautiful results of these efforts—a year or more was sometimes spent in copying one manuscript—should be appreciated by all students of information science.

Early libraries were small, and manuscripts expensive; the books, kept in cupboards or chests, were chained to desks when in use. To facilitate information retrieval, books were arranged by subject or kind—e.g., religious, secular, Greek, or Latin. Catalogs were first rough check lists on which, later, descriptions of contents were given.

Responsibility for "higher education" gradually shifted from the monasteries (chiefly theological studies) to the cathedral schools (study of Latin grammar and, later, of vernacular writings) and thence to the medieval university. The university was also the local book dealer—a necessity to guarantee the authenticity of texts, which were copied by scribes and rented to students. Gradually each college within a university came to have its own library, with books divided by accession and according to subject. Books were now sometimes stored on shelves rather than in chests. More important works were still chained to desks, though with longer chains that enabled students to take them to tables and sit down while studying.

By the 15th century, people of the middle classes were able to own books, thanks to affordable paper, the invention of the printing press with movable type, and the spread of writings in various vernaculars. Better papers, inks, and printing techniques then led to the rapid evolution (by about 1700) of the printed book in its usual present form, including title page, illustrations, contents pages, and index. The presses stimulated and broadcast the results of intellectual curiosity, helped create the "professional way of letters" (Gates, 1962, p. 21), made possible the success of the Reformation, and by means of the printed map hastened the era of discovery and exploration.

INFORMATION TRANSFER DURING THE MODERN ERA

During the 16th century, book coverings and content varied greatly. Printing types gradually ceased to be copies of manuscript writing and assumed an identity all their own. Periodicals appeared, followed by the first modern encyclopedia in 1630 and by newspapers later in the century. In the 19th century, technology produced clothbound books printed in four colors on paper manufactured from wood pulp. Copyright legislation was enacted, and guarantees (or lack thereof) of a free press became very important.

Between 1500 and 1900 many important European libraries appeared. These included: the Laurentian Library (Florence), the Ambrosian Library (Milan), the Vatican Library, the Bibliotheque Nationale in Paris (open twice a week to the public since 1692, when it was already older than all but a few American libraries are today), Oxford and Cambridge University libraries, the British Museum Library, the Austrian Royal Library, and the university libraries at Ghent and Lourain. Several outstanding German state and university libraries were also founded during that time. During that same time, circulating libraries with cataloged inventories, popular reading rooms, and children's collections began to appear.

The first American colleges (Harvard, 1638; William & Mary, 1695; Yale, 1700; Princeton, 1736) began as, or were founded in association with, gifts of books (Yale with only 40). By 1725, Harvard's collection had grown to 3000.[4] However, until almost a century ago, library books were often difficult for students to get at. Some college libraries were open only an hour per fortnight. Some libraries classified books into three broad categories: memory, judgment, and imagination; or history, philosophy, and poetry. The significance of using any subject-matter-oriented classification system cannot be overstated; this was an opening wedge toward developing access systems that were to become easy to use by virtually anyone. In other libraries books were arranged according to appearance, accession, or donor (Gates, 1962, p. 23).

The Library of Congress, established in 1809, was reestablished in 1815 after being burned by the British the year before. A tax-supported library appeared in 1833, in Peterborough, New Hampshire. Dewey's first *Decimal Classification* was published in 1876, and the American Library Association was founded the same year. By 1960, more than two thousand institutions of higher education in the United States possessed libraries containing about 167 million volumes.

A brief review of some of the factors that distinguish the recent past (say through World War II) from the present seems in order. While the nature of information hasn't changed, our attitudes toward it have. We now are much more protective over virtually every definable datum (a piece of information, a single point in a large collection of data), and want to be able to store, manipulate, resequence, and retrieve economically and quickly any conceivable combination of data. While the uses of such assembled data are manifold and extend into every legitimate and illegitimate endeavor of humankind, such expectations were totally without reason until the advent of the computer.

The computer is basically a machine that makes very simple, relatively error-free mathematical tests (comparisons) and calculations. It makes them exceedingly fast and, if properly programmed and maintained, without losing what it has committed to its "memory." While this may appear elementary (and it is), it has far-reaching significance. It frees its human "master" to contemplate the information transfer needed and to prepare unambiguous instructions ("programs"). The computer then unemotionally carries out the orders given it. When all is going as it should, those orders are executed 100% replicably, an unthinkable attainment for human operations. When we program it correctly, the computer neither loses patience nor memory. Because of the computer's capacious memory, it can build virtually unlimited data bases (stored information) that may be retrieved from "IBM cards," magnetic tapes and discs, holographic devices, and the like. Entire technologies for ancillary equipment (hardware) and software (programs) now develop continuously. Theoretical research continues to accelerate toward improved economies, faster "switching time" speeds, more rapid location of filed information, more units of information stored in smaller areas or volumes of storage medium, more accurate data transmissibility, and the like.

Think about some of the gains and losses as the passing of information has gone from, say, the chanted epic to the humming and clicking electronic print out of hundreds of characters per second in variously ordered matrices of at least partly useful data displays. Is it progress? What new problems do you suppose are carried in on the heels of the emerging technologies?

INFORMATION TRANSFER TODAY:
MAGNITUDE OF THE TASK

Fingerprints and income tax records; social security records and records of human exploration of space. What have these in common?

They are all part of the billions of bits of data handled routinely today that were not even part of the record until this century.

Add certain medical records, credit bureau data and credit card transactions, community and industrial environmental pollution data, meteorological readings, patent information, and so forth, and the breadth of the data storage and retrieval problem begins to become clear. Further:

- The federal government produces billions of pieces of paper per year—many of them decrying the inexorable spread of the "paper blitz."
- Military engineering documentation costing several billion dollars each year results, among other things, in billions of new engineering drawings.
- Space scientists grapple daily with the problem of securely storing lunar samples and data about them, as well as information from other interplanetary missions and from artificial satellites—some dealing with quantities at the microgram or smaller scale, and many needing to be selectively available to authorized personnel only, and without delay.
- Millions of technical articles are published every year in more than 50 languages.
- Some 50–100 million checks pass through U.S. banks every working day, each being handled some 5 or 6 times.

It is quite clear that libraries, many with collections of several million books and periodicals, are not alone in facing information transfer problems. Other kinds of data that are dealt with regularly include: commercial and governmental list maintenance operations, some with lists numbering tens of millions of entries; voluminous medical records, including hand written reports and strip-chart printouts; millions of service records, such as those kept by the U.S. Veteran's Administration; hundreds of millions of insurance policies and billions of legal agreements, and untold numbers of court rulings and decisions. In addition, U.S. law enforcement and emergency agencies serving some 20 thousand municipalities are interconnected via special services that must deal with incomplete data patterns, for the most part; also, strategic military data must be instantly and unerringly available for purposes of national security.

The commercial and military response to this proliferation of data has been a steady development of techniques for automation of documentation and retrieval functions. And this is what much of this chapter is all about.[5] Literally thousands of indexing and abstracting services attempt to provide access to the growing pools of selected data within this sea of recorded information. Additionally, there are thousands of specialized information collecting centers in the United States and throughout the world. Much of the published literature simply cannot be touched by all of these services.

INFORMATION TRANSFER TODAY: ITS CHALLENGES

Organizational, technological, and strategic challenges face the specialists who are now pushing the frontier of information transfer into the future. For example, information transfer must be planned on a system-wide basis: the larger the better, in many cases. Larger systems generally require greater staff. When many people work with the system, access to it must be made very simple, but simplicity of access endangers system security (e.g., in military or banking applications, and personnel records). Dealing satisfactorily with these factors drives the cost of the system upward. High costs necessitate a back-up system (a fail-safe mechanism where lives or property may be involved) or back-up records (e.g., daily microfilming of all records being run for all accounts of large businesses, these to replace previous back-up tapes or films and to be stored apart—usually in a bank vault). Such protection drives the costs even higher and gives even more people access to the sensitive parts of the system, and on and on. . . .

The Challenge of Indexing

Another view of the challenge is provided by indexers. Indexing problems can be caused by many factors. These could include indexer training and background, inherent ambiguity in the indexing system, widely varying significance of indexable elements in the system (and thus a wide range of responses to those elements by the human indexer), and variations in the jargon of the originators of the items to be indexed or of the indexer or both. These factors can cause difficulties whether the indexing system is a manual punched-card system or a modern office/laboratory installation of a system-wide data processing computer terminal. Indexing and retrieval problems include: loss of filed material (misplacement is the same as loss when irretrievability results), difficulty in file-structure modification following original design specification or critieria (i.e., can the system handle new variables?), and operator loss of familiarity with file contents or subject matter.

The last item listed above is hardly trivial. The best librarians in a traditional library are those who not only understand the operating guidelines of their institutions, but also know where to look for needed items quickly—often without reference to card catalogs or similar tools of the trade. Indexers and abstractors today sometimes operate strictly on a mechanical basis—for example from keywords or from camera-ready abstracts provided by authors—and understand little or nothing about the materials they handle.

The extent to which those problems occur will, of course, depend at least in part upon the size and complexity of the system being used to index or abstract information.

The many different indexing systems devised to make information available to users range from simple personalized systems to complex computer-dependent systems. Fenner[6] described a system for information storage and retrieval that relied on a reader to prepare index card sets: one with citation, abstract, and personal accession number; the other with an index of relevant terms, each with accession numbers of indexed works that contain information relevant to the particular term. The first set would be filed by accession number, the second by alphabetic sequence. Herner and Vellucci's 1972 book[7] exemplified the other end of the range. It describes, verbally and graphically, only 35 systems in federal use. It was prepared in cooperation with a panel of the federally-supported Committee on Scientific and Technical Information and is so complex that flow charts are required to understand it fully.

The Challenge of Transition

A different challenge is that encountered by the Library of Congress (LC) as it prepares to move into the next millenium. Innumerable problems are inherent in curating holdings that at the end of 1978 numbered nearly 75 million, of which nearly 19 million were books and pamphlets. In addition to categorizing all its inventory, being the patent and copyright repository for the United States, and a host of other services, the LC is an important information disseminating resource. Its Congressional Research Service, for example, answered some 300,000 congressional telephone inquiries in 1978— up to 2000 calls per day.

Here's one way in which LC has modernized: printed duplicates of LC catalog cards have been available for purchase by other libraries since 1901. This service resulted in an incredibly large inventory and a correspondingly huge search problem. In September of 1978 LC's Card Automated Reproduction Demand System (CARDS) was introduced. CARDS does away with the inventory. By using laser technology, a computer, and xerographic techniques, catalog cards are now printed on demand; orders are now filled more quickly.

Given the volume of our rapidly expanding world literature, even the finest details of cataloging are significant. LC's response, rescheduled now for January 1981, is a planned switch from a manual to a machine cataloging system. Implementation of this second catalog requires two things (assuming that the people and machines are ready): (1) the present catalog must be "frozen;" and, (2) an evolved set of rules must be put into effect—the *Anglo-American Catalog Rules*, second edition (referred to as AACR2 by the Library of Congress), which has also been endorsed by the national libraries of Australia, Canada and Great Britain. The *Library of Congress Information Bulletin*[8] discussed some of the problems associated with making the anticipated changes. Most users will little appreciate the vexing problems associated with making such a major switch, but the long-term effects should include improved services.

The Challenges of Distribution and Standardization

It should be quite evident that there is no single solution to all aspects of the information transfer problem, else it would long ago have been uniformly and universally implemented. Evolving information transfer creates problems that are not easily solved: users want all the "new information" instantaneously once they've discovered their need for it; and, the energy, money, and labor costs of retooling systems and trying to make various components compatible with each other are enormous.

Problems abound when users assume they know (1) what they want and (2) how they can gain access to it. In light of the tremendous increase of printed information in science and technology, and of a corresponding reduced distribution for that information (even within the "invisible colleges" comprised of the primary researchers within any particular scientific or technological subspecialty), neither of these assumptions is necessarily valid. Thus, while we see journal titles increasing in number, their distribution in some cases is dwindling, and in others is not proportional to growth in the population of scientists.

According to Martin M. Cummings[9], a model provided by the MEDLINE system speaks quite eloquently to the need to identify the information one is seeking. Through MEDLINE a million on-line ("while you wait") searches are performed each year; economical and rapid searches of the biomedical literature are made from remote computer terminals all around the country, queries being directed to a centralized computer facility located in Bethesda, Maryland. Cummings noted the need for library consortia, linked via computer indexing services (with union catalogs available), to enable the retrieval of identified articles. Again, he cited the biomedical model as a good one to follow.

Others have declared the need for standardized approaches that would give evolving systems certain points in common—an absolutely essential ingredient for machine-based systems. Information transfer systems changes must be based on constructed common denominators; these are needed to link systems. And, they must take into account the millions upon millions of dollars that have gone into systems design by governmental agencies, by national and international groups, by private industry, by academic institutions, libraries, and so on. Each is looking for a "best" solution for its own circumstances.

Even if it were possible to arrive at a universal "best" system, theoreticians must recognize that tomorrow's "best" will be "better" than today's (though undoubtedly "worse" for some users). Moreover, high-volume users typically modify existing computer software (programs) to better suit their particular needs and hardware (machine) configurations.

As with most records systems, when we alter our computer technology "the good we do lives after us." Every change we make must be documented. Changes instituted today may affect all records existing prior to date of implementation. Should we retain a separate system for prior records, or should they all be converted/translated? [By whom and at what cost borne by whom: And at what cost if not done or considered?] Criteria of cost effectiveness for systems old and new must be the same through time; otherwise the user may gain little from the changes made.

National Science Foundation funding during the mid- to late-1970s of a project entitled *Improving the Dissemination of Scientific and Technical Information* underscored the importance of this subject. A large collection of data and technique descriptions was published. This highlighted both the rapid evolution of information transfer systems and the desirability of standardization.

On Computerized Improvements in Information Transfer

Computer technology is not the only form of improved information transfer. Discoveries in presentational format may also help meet the enormous challenge. For example, it has been found that (owing to the word-shape loss) material printed in upper case letters only is much harder to read than the normal mixture with lower case letters (editors declare that "all caps is no caps"). Further, a 20–24 pica line (3-1/2 to 4 inches) is the easiest line length to read in a book. For greatest legibility, brown ink should be applied to light brown or buff pages; serifs should be retained on letters; cursive fonts should be avoided. For retrieval ease (especially by machine), some calendar standards call for year, month, then day citations, e.g., 19811105, for 5 November 1981. A bibliographic citation standard takes an entire publication (ANSI Z39.29-1977) to describe. And to minimize the easiest place for errors to occur in a typical scientific or technical publication, literature citations should include the entire journal title. Yet, how many of these admonitions are usually followed? Why are they ignored? How about tables of contents for journals? A most useful format separates—by column organization and type style— authors' names, starting page number, and paper titles; why do so few journals adopt these changes?

Change comes so very slowly. Sometimes it should. Always it should be adopted with caution.

INFORMATION TRANSFER TODAY: SOME APPLICATIONS

Government Data Banks

Reflecting on the thousands of observations made every second concerning all conceivable aspects of our environment, Hall[10] noted that most data enter one or more federal data banks. Examples of such systems and their data types include:

1. *National Water Resources Data System*—data needed for decisions affecting water development, land management, pollution control, environmental enhancement, flood and drought protection, etc., are continuously acquired from nearly 5700 sites throughout the country, and from 18,000 streamflow stations, 28,000 observation wells, and aerial investigations (in 1972 alone, 860 aerial investigations, covering about 3/4 million square miles were in progress) (for information: Chief Hydrologist, Water Resources Division, U.S. Geological Survey, Reston, Virginia).

2. *Earth Resources Observations System (EROS) Data Center*— collects photographic products acquired by NASA from surface, airborne, or space-borne platforms (for information: EROS Data Center, Sioux Falls, South Dakota).

3. *NASA-Processed Earth Resources Technology Satellite (ERTS)*—processes and disseminates its imagery and that of aircraft and spacecraft in support of Earth Resources Survey Program (this imagery, as well as that from USAS and other NASA efforts, is available from the EROS Data Center).

4. *Other aerial photographs and imagery* may be obtained through other agencies, such as, National Oceanographic and Atmospheric Administration (NOAA), United States Department of Agriculture (USDA) (National Climatic Center, Department of Conservation).

5. *National Water Quality Control Information System (STORET)*—is a computer-based repository for all Envi-

ronmental Protection Agency water quality data, which in 1972 had a storage capacity of about 2 billion alphanumeric data characters (EPA, Washington, D.C.).

6. *National Oceanographic Data Center (NODC)*—collects marine data from the world over, and makes them available through over a dozen different data dissemination services;

7. *National Geophysical and Solar-Terrestrial Data Center (NGSDC)*—collects data about seismology, geomagnetism, marine geology and geophysics, solar activity, interplanetary phenomena, the ionosphere, cosmic rays, aurorae, and airglow. For starters, this includes about 300,000 seismograms and some 50,000 magnetograms per year.

8. *Office of Energy Information Services' (OEIS) National Energy Information Center (NEIC)*—has a telephone information service to answer energy questions quickly, whether asked by governmental agencies, academic institutions, commercial organizations, or the general public (NEIC, Washington, D.C.).

9. *Federal Energy Data Index (FEDEX)*—is a computerized bibliographic search file giving quick reference to Energy Information Administration (EIA) publications (Department of Energy Technical Information Center, also USERLINE System of Bibliographic Retrieval Services, Scotia, N.Y.).

Nongovernmental Applications

Among current nongovernmental systems, ERIC (the Educational Resources Information Center) is a network of clearinghouses designed to provide easier access to the literature on education. It maintains document reproduction services and publishes *Resources in Education* and *Current Index to Journals in Education* (both of which are best used in conjunction with the *Thesaurus of ERIC Descriptors*).

In his 1971 "Citation Indexes,"[11] Marvin Weinstock detailed the function of his company's services. By 1973 he claimed (in an informal talk) his company's *Science Citation Index* already covered 90% of the world's significant scientific literature by including 2500 primary journals from 41 nations. Since then the *Index* has grown considerably. As a rationale for such an index Weinstock cites identification of relationships among documents, ease of nonmachine indexing that doesn't require subject-matter specialists, currency of resulting indexes, and invulnerability to scientific and technological obsolescence. (Citation indexing assumes that article writers cite earlier pertinent work in much the same way, perhaps, that precedents are cited in legal texts.) The interdisciplinary source lists that result from a citation index are marvelous aids to researchers in fields other than the primary one in which an author may have published. Weinstock (p. 37) claimed that "citation indexes can now perform important evaluative, analytical, and predictive roles that were never imagined for subject indexes."

Professional organizations during the past decade have proposed the means to "capture" the entire literature of some specified kind, usually for easier—whether free or tariffed—access by a larger clientele and less redundancy in the searching process. In one proposal of this sort, the American Geological Institute[12] proposed a system to include at least 11 kinds of information sources: (1) formal meetings and symposia; (2) primary journals and monographs; (3) translations and review journals; (4) bibliographies, abstract journals, and indexes; (5) archival holdings of libraries; (6) guidebooks and informal reports; (7) theses and dissertations; (8) data collections; (9) glossaries and thesauri; (10) maps, charts and photographs; and, (11) collections of interest to geoscientists (type specimens, cores, well logs, thin sections, mineral and fossil samples, etc.).

Other Forms of Progress

At the Open University and other places in the United Kingdom, computer-based equipment allows wide-ranging information/teaching dialogs through telephone-connected computer/typewriter terminals coordinated with publicly accessible television channels. Beyond the stage of experimentation of the British system is the University of Illinois' PLATO, with its own computer programming language. PLATO relies less on up-to-the-minute, system-wide data, but allows fully illustrated (full-color) branching, interactive, programmed lessons to be handled by its computer-managed network. It is effective for pre-schoolers and university students alike, regardless where in this country their PLATO terminal is located.

Technology and consumer demand now allow similar systems— with virtually equivalent power—to be purchased or leased for home or office use at surprisingly low costs. Such systems are useful for time management, business accounting, selective daily news scanning, and a multitude of other functions, as well as for writing and editing. Books are here to stay, but microforms are becoming more important; the trend is toward universal indexing systems and individualized computer-managed systems for input/output[13]. However automated things get, though, good writing, proper citations, and good editing remain important. If they are not done right the first time, before input to automatic equipment, much of the speed, economy, and power of technological advances will be wasted.

Direct to Print

Information systems such as computer-based indexing and bibliographic services are moving rapidly toward custom designing for each user or each specific problem. Several services (for example, Lockheed's DIALOG) have multiple/cumulative data bases from which all information is computer extractable—printable in any of several individualized formats.

Applying these modern technologies, at least one science publisher, who sells separates of individual papers, uses the record of each sale as feedback to refine an extensive computer-managed profile of customers. The profile makes it possible to determine closely how many copies of a given paper will sell, enabling the publisher to make accurate print orders, reduce postage costs, and optimize storage space.

With help from word processors and computerized composition systems, customized textbooks are now being assembled and printed in press runs as small as a few hundred. It is even possible to prepare your own manuscript in OCR (optical character recognition) machine-readable typing characters, from which an automated system can produce a bound copy.

Because technological advances reduce response time, the traditional print methods may lose ground to other forms. Many people believe that microforms lack only a good portable reader/printer to displace print. Condensed size and new retrieval methods certainly promise saved time and money, as well as enhanced capability.

INFORMATION TRANSFER TOMORROW: PROJECTED TECHNOLOGIES AND DEMANDS

It now seems likely that by the end of this century writers and editors will be dealing with microforms as primary bibliographic tools and documents, with documents that are largely converted to machine-readable forms, with automatic indexing and titling, with machine-produced citations, and even with automatically produced documents. Even now, before Orwell's targeted 1984, the above is true in many situations.

Even now, a manuscript can be stored on tape or on a floppy disc, then recalled paragraph-by-paragraph on the television-like screen of a word processor (a minicomputer with a rather specialized microprocessor element designed for editing functions). An editor can select any line on the screen and correct, rewrite, relocate, or delete it from the text. The editor can add type specifications, and within hours the entire manuscript can be made ready for the photographic process that leads to publication. Presswork and binding operations have been automated; paper goes into one end of the book-making machinery, and bound copies come out the other.

Still seeking the ideal model, scientists are trying to anticipate needs and solutions beyond the day-after-tomorrow. Writing in *Science*[14] Thomas H. Maugh, II, provided a glimpse into the future. As an example of the great need to find better data-storage methods, he cited the information coming to us from NASA satellites and probes. From them we are now annually receiving 1000 trillion data bits each year, of which some 10 terabits ($=10 \times 10^{12}$ coded pieces of information) will be added to storage for at least 50 years. Private industry now stores some 265 billion financial documents, and our government stores some 20 million cubic feet of records. (Maugh concluded that in 1980 information storage should be a $2 billion [1978 dollars] business.)

According to Maugh, one terabit of information, at 800 bits per punched card stored in boxes of 2000 cards, would fill a string of boxes 123 miles long. Magnetic tape stores data more compactly, one reel being the equivalent of about 677 boxes of punched cards, with the disadvantage, however, that it will deteriorate in some 10–15 years. In a carefully controlled environment, these tapes can be cared for at a cost of about $10 per reel per year, or about $1 million per terabit library. A microfiche can hold about 1.5 megabits of information, or the equivalent of about 1560 punched cards. Ultrafiches can store the contents of 12–15 fiches. Thus, Maugh envisions a terabit fiche library 777 feet long. His solution to this ungainliness is to go to "holofiches," which are experimental storage devices. Each 4″ × 6″ holofiche can store 200 megabits of information in 20,000 individual holograms, thus holding as much information as 208,000 punched cards. He envisions a cost of 50¢ per holofiche.

Meanwhile, computer technology progresses toward smaller, faster, more able, more reliable, and cheaper hardware. Lessened energy demands and greater processing speeds make smaller computers more desirable, but there are limits—physical constraints—upon the effective miniaturization that can occur. These limits are determined in part by the speed of light, i.e., the speed at which an electric impulse can travel. Consider, as Lewis Branscomb[15] does for example, a future need to compute at a "rate of ten machine cycles per nanosecond [$= 1 \times 10^{-10}$ sec] . . . [that] is 50 times the speed of the fastest computer today . . . [and] face the fact that an electrical signal can travel . . . only about 3 centimeters . . . in 1/10 nanosecond. To avoid deleterious transmission delays we would have to fit all the circuits into a hypothetical computer no bigger than a 1-inch cube . . ." (p. 144). For full functioning, such a computer might need some 300,000 circuits—which in turn would create a severe heat-dissipation problem, as its estimated kilowatt of power is about as much as now operates an ordinary 2-slice toaster.

Hence a new technology is needed to replace silicon and analogous technologies currently in use. That new technology might well be the so-called Josephson technology, which takes advantage of metals' superconductivity when cooled to 4.2°K. Individual experimental devices have already been demonstrated that have switching speeds of 5×10^{-14} sec; today's best computers switch in the 1 picosecond (1×10^{-12} sec) range. Thus a computer built on the Josephson technology promises to be very small, very fast, very cold, and—at least to begin with—very expensive.

Can you imagine a complete computer small enough to hold in your hand . . . *and* the volume then required for its cooling systems, not to mention other support systems?

Turning his attention to computer memory, Branscomb converts his estimate of 20 million books in the Library of Congress (LC) into 9 $\times 10^{12}$ letters, or about 70 trillion bits (20 million books $\times$ 300 pages $\times$ 1500 letters). Today's IBM 3850 mass storage system holds 3.8 $\times 10^{12}$ bits, or more than a twentieth of the LC total. Making a point by means of absurd extrapolations to a century hence, Branscomb relates computer storage growth capacity and population growth, and concludes that the same investment that would hold 20 million books in magnetic storage today would finance 15 billion libraries— or one for each person he expects will then be living. Further extrapolations: Computers may cost under a penny in 2080, and may be biological, patterned after DNA molecules.

Input/output modes will also be subject to major changes. Voice recognition and word pattern recognition are already a limited experimental reality. Similarly, non-impact printer technologies are already here in the form of ink jet printing and printing by laser electrophotography.

Branscomb assumes that various information technologies, such as typewriters, television, movies, telephones, radio, records, and tapes will become interrelated and interchangeable. Given the rates of technological growth, he even considers that it may be cheaper 100 years from now to reconstitute or reacquire information from basic elements each time rather than to store it. Even today many mathematical tables can be quickly generated by, or programmed into, a sophisticated hand-held calculator as needed.

Communications technology already has given us the benefit of data acquisition services, such as DIALOG. Laser technology can now carry 800 simultaneous conversations through a hair-thin optical fiber—translated into data bits, a transmission rate of some 40,000 books per hour. Eventually, writes Branscomb (p. 146), optical technology is expected to transfer data equivalent to a billion books per second; and, light-wave communication could well do away with the need for wire connections between terminals.

INFORMATION TRANSFER TOMORROW: POSSIBLE SOCIAL EFFECTS

Since the news-covering media today affect the news they report, the significance of their role in the public dissemination of science will continue to grow. Similarly, the popularization of scientists' roles on TV programs and in the cinema may have as much impact as "real science."[16]

In an elaborate report printed in 1971[17], UNESCO workers made recommendations (p. 1) "concerned with the cultivation of this resource [scientific information], and with increasing its accessibility and use to the end that, as an international resource, it may contribute optimally to the scientific, educational, social, cultural, and economic development of all countries." Recommendations are addressed to governments, scientific organizations, and technical experts professionally concerned with the operation of science information services. In arguing the necessity of a worldwide resource, the *UNISIST* document shows how such a system may help to prevent an information monopoly—intellectual, technical, financial—from becoming concentrated in the hands of a few. The need for prevention is related to the doubling times for global knowledge and the resulting costs of handling scientific and technical information.[18]

Lewis M. Branscomb[19], as vice-president and chief scientist of the International Business Machines Corporation, put future prospects into a different perspective. He distinguished information from other important commodities, like food and energy, by noting (1) its increasing surplus rather than shortage, and (2) the fact that the more one has, the easier it becomes to get even more. As with other commodities, timely and equitable distribution of information is desirable. The key to its proper management, Branscomb concluded, is the computer, though software will be needed that is friendlier to human users. He underscores that having data and information or knowledge or wisdom is quite different from being able to communicate it. "By taking over knowledge distribution, electronic information systems will let universities concentrate on new knowledge. More importantly, they will expand everyone's right to information and free expression through the existing media system and to protection from misuse of information by others" (p. 143).

QUESTIONS FOR STUDY AND DISCUSSION

Having just read a smattering of views about information exchange from its earliest known written beginnings to a hypothetical century-ahead time, you should be ready to apply some relevant notions to your own circumstances and interests.

It might be evident to some readers that the processes of preparing storable information are in many ways becoming more important than the process of storing it. This allusion to "junk information," perhaps analogous to "junk food," also suggests the increased ease with which we can get at information. These questions do not have *a* right answer but logical responses are expected.[20]

Information

In its smallest and most essential form, information can be regarded as a sensory signal, a fact, or a feeling that can be perceived or communicated. We continually receive information—whether or not it is processed further, either consciously or unconsciously. Moreover, information *is* information whether or not it is at the moment retrievable. Information need only have the potential for retrieval.

In order to be received or conveyed, information must exist in a perceptible form or code. Information may be generated and perceived by one or more of our senses, aided or unaided.

Think about the rôle of each of our senses in perceiving or processing information. List in the space below all the ways you can imagine that sensory information may be carried; in so doing, reconsider what information is. You may either classify your response, or answer with individually listed items. Classification, if used, may be according to information type or style, to senses involved in the information transfer, to code mode, etc.

You may have classified your list according to our senses—singly or in combination. A few examples are listed below:

Sight

Books, movies, film strips, microfiches, microfilm, microform, displays, documents, indexes, film loops, maps, games (strategy), journals, pamphlets, TV/videotapes, films [note that several of these items overlap with at least one other sense]

Sound

Records, movies, audiotapes, film-strip records, cassettes

Touch

Manual: braille books, raised relief maps, games (strategy). Other tactile inputs: teeth to determine particle size of small grains of sand or silt or clay

Smell

Odors/aromas/perfumes

Taste

Food types, certain crystals

Extra-Sensory

Clairvoyance

You may have responded to this question in terms of categories of things, such as:

Signals

Smoke signals, morse code, electroencephalograph tracings

Specimens

Rocks, insects, leaves, signatures

Are the following *all* examples of information? Graphs, charts, tables, photographs, works of art; collections of stamps, coins, or just about anything else; fingerprints; nature trails; meteorological conditions; discussion groups/meetings (agendas, conclusions, and so forth); attendance data; medical and dental records; fossils; radio; elemental or isotopic composition; telescopic observation; symptoms; hydrographic data, such as salinity, pH, Eh; blood types; body language signals; slide collections; X-ray tomography patterns; polygraphs; holographs; nuclear information; telephone numbers; traffic signals; cellular information—dead and living; chemical formulae; binary bits and computer bytes; morphological subdivisions; rope trail; classifications; coded indexes, . . . and many more.

It should not be very difficult, at this point, to recognize the universality of the notion *information*. Can you find anything to exclude from its scope?

Information Management Systems

You have just considered some of the many forms information can take. To be useful in information transfer, a system is needed that groups it together, stores it, and makes it accessible. Consider your list from the first question, or the items listed in the foregoing discussion. Relate them to their appropriate management systems. Examples are given. You will note that depending on your perspective, the last two columns in the example (and in your work) may be switched under their headings. What are the different kinds of retrieval systems, and for what kind of information might each system be ideally suited?

Forms of information	System to manage them	Retrieval systems
insect specimens	museum cases	entymological taxonomy key
microform document	coded index	dial-access reader/printer

Factors Used to Assess Information Systems
What factors would you use to assess a system's effectiveness for
information transfer—i.e., for the grouping, storing, and accessing of
information? Generalize your answer unless you have a particular
system in mind, in which case it should be identified. One example is
given.

Factor   *Brief definition or clarifying statement*

scope   The system can group, store, and access all information to
           be placed into it.

The following are among the factors that should be considered before committing yourself to an information transfer system; simplicity for operator, for user, for storer; reliability, including uniformity or universality of language; constancy or internal consistency; efficiency, in terms of time, energy, and other costs; accessibility, including different categories for different kinds of system users; (sequenceability)—ordering or classification used or potentially available; durability of the system, its components, its interface, or its output; retrievability, whether user oriented; editorial/editing capacity; capacity (volume of information the system can handle); flexibility; administration (management/control factors); precision; conciseness; accuracy; completeness; (interfaceability) (with other systems); ease of maintenance, and cost factors associated with same; storage: types, size, capacity, physical space to house the system and its output; quality of product; privacy and security (selectively); standardization; selectivity; currency and ability to update; speed; scope; development (including improvement of system) time and cost and energy; transmissability; and, entry/maintenance costs: time, energy, money, labor.

Application/Evaluation

Assess the systems previously identified with reference to the factors also previously listed. In the process, you may think of systems and factors other than those you or the text listed; include them also. There are at least two ways to respond to this charge. In the first, devise a means of theoretically assessing each factor as it could be applied to each system. A person might then use your evaluation scheme on any information storage/retrieval (ISR) system he/she might imagine or need. In the second, think of either a present ISR need you have, or a possible situation in the future—say, in ten years—and design/define the ISR system you will/would use/adapt for your purpose, giving a rationale that indicates your consideration of other systems and many relevant factors. Write your answer so that it could help resolve a real ISR problem. Given the rate at which technology is modifying the information transfer field and its applications, the answer to this question no doubt differs significantly from one you might have given only a year or two ago. In essence, you should focus here on a particular problem—or a class of problems—that relates to your work or interests and be able to propose a systematic solution for plausible implementation. Who knows: if you think hard enough about it, you may devise a solution that will benefit you for years. (Some of our students have had that experience.)

Additional Study Questions

In a text that seeks specific answers to most questions it poses, there should also be room for food-for-thought questions.

How do you think the phenomenon of "future shock" will affect information transfer or its purveyors or users?

What effects on society did the advent of writing have? Can you think of analogs to that quantum leap?

Of what major cultural and social significance was the appearance of the book? How did it improve upon oral transmission of information, or recording of data on papyri or clay tablets?

In what way did classification systems for printed information represent a breakthrough in communications? What were their effects on access to information?

What did libraries accomplish that no other institution could? And when did that begin to happen?

What will the next information transfer revolution involve? (Or will it be an evolution?)

Picture our world today without xerography, photography, and electronic data processing (especially word processing). What would happen in a time of sustained power outage? How can we guard against the effects of power blackouts?

How would the "invisible college" function if information storage systems should become filled? Surely new information would still "happen." What then?

NOTES

1. Much of the historical information in this section was excerpted and modified from Jean Key Gates' 1962 book, *Guide to the use of books and libraries* (New York, McGraw-Hill, pp. 3–25), which also has an excellent relevant bibliography (pp. 25–27).

2. See Carlos Castaneda's *The Teachings of Don Juan: A Yaqui Way of Knowledge*, 1969, New York, Ballantine Books, Inc., 276 pp., for a modern-day example of this in the western world.

3. A recent development of the greatest interest to scholars—many of whom believe that its importance will overshadow that of the Dead Sea Scrolls of Qumran— is the discovery of a huge cache of at least 15,000 tablets at Ebla in Syria. They may be more than four millenia old, and could substantiate several Old Testament stories, verify the existence of persons mentioned in the Bible, and modify our dating of several critically important events of biblical times (the Patriarchal Period, especially).

4. By way of contrast, the Association of Research Libraries shows 1978–1979 holdings of Harvard to include over 9.9 million volumes and 95,000 current serials. Yale, the second largest university library, has 7.2 million volumes and 57,740 current serials. Princeton ranks 18th among Association member libraries. Among other U.S. libraries, only the Library of Congress (LC) exceeds Harvard's collection (LC's holdings: 18.9 million volumes; 76,583 current serials). New York's public library system is only behind LC in the public domain, and with 4.9 million volumes and 161,011 current serials is larger than Columbia University's—ranking behind only Harvard, Yale, U. Illinois, U. California (Berkeley) and U. Indiana.

5. For one account of an interesting—and suspensefully written—application of those techniques, read Frederick Forsythe's *The Day of the Jackal*, 1971, Bantam edition (1973), New York, Bantam Books, 495 pp.

6. *Journal of Geological Education* (1964, pp. 94–97)

7. *Selected Federal Computer-Based Information Systems*, Washington, D.C., Information Resources Press.

8. 3 March 1978 (pp. 152–156), "Freezing the Library of Congress Catalog."

9. *Science*, "Information Transfer: The Biomedical Model," 1978, vol. 202 (n.4374), p. 1247.

10. *Federal Environmental Data Centers and Systems*, 1972, unpublished preprint: Cincinnati, Ohio, National Environmental Information Symposium, September 24–27, p. 30.

11. *Encyclopedia of Library and Information Science*, New York, Marcel Dekker, Inc., v. 5, pp. 16–40.

12. 1971, "Geoscience Information," *Geotimes*, v. 16(3), p. 19.

13. Wendell Cochran, Peter Fenner, and Mary Hill, *eds.*, 1979 *Geowriting*, 3rd ed., American Geological Institute, Falls Church, Va. p. 79.

14. "Holographic Filing: An Industry on the Verge of Birth," vol. 201, pp. 431–432.

15. Lewis M. Branscomb, 1979, "Information: the Ultimate Frontier," *Science*, v. 203, pp. 143–147.

16. *Science in the Newspaper*, published by the American Association for the Advancement of Science in 1974 (Norman Metzger, ed.), gave us a glimpse of the future through the eyes of speculative science reporters.

17. *UNISIST*, especially pp. 1–3, 9–21, 26, 133–145, Paris, UNESCO.

18. Successive information doublings: from the time of Christ to 1750, then to 1900, then 1950, then 1960. Seen another way, the number of scientific workers has increased ten-fold every 50 years for more than 2800 years. Where there were 1000 scientists in 1800, there were 10,000 in 1850, 100,000 in 1900, and 1,000,000 in 1950. By contrast, U.S. federal expenditures on scientific and technical information were about $150 million in 1963, $175 million in 1964, $200 million in 1965, $380 million in 1966, and more than $500 million for 1968 (*UNISIST*, 1971, p. 11).

19. Op. cit.

20. You may be making several passes at these questions: the first time, cold; the second time, after the readings; and third time after reading some of the cited literature, other references you've found on your own, and commercial sales literature. Finally, during a seminar if you have such a discussion, there will be a fourth opportunity to revise your answers.

INTRODUCTION

This chapter gives you an opportunity to apply what you have learned about various practical aspects of information transfer, including locating stored information. It can help you prepare and annotate bibliographies; it can also help you compile and cite primary data from the literature. You are also asked to gain some familiarity with today's copyright laws while you are preparing two rather different bibliographies.

Sound and successful research in any field will depend upon your ability to research the literature, evaluate what you find, extract the data you need, and give appropriate credit to your sources. Earlier exercises in this book have led you through the reference section of your library, enabling you to find specified bits of information. Understanding a body of information involves reading in its primary literature.

The first exercise in this chapter requires you to prepare an annotated bibliography covering an area relevant to your studies or interests. Should you be working under someone's supervision for this exercise, get approval of your proposed bibliography topic before you begin the work; the idea is to select a topic of appropriate scope—neither too select, nor too universal. You will want to exhaust the literature within a reasonable number of citations. It is also helpful to find a knowledgeable critic who can evaluate your bibliographic entries and annotations, perhaps even checking on your progress shortly after you've begun the work, and again prior to final typing. Your bibliography should be comprehensive for the topic selected. Make sure that it is current. Include as many pre-primary and primary sources as you can find. Peruse all the materials you cite. Your annotations should be of substance, not mere repetitions of titles. Typically 50–75 words each, they must be based on your own reading and comprehension of the works cited.

Type your bibliography on standard size and quality typing paper and use a consistent citation style.

If you are submitting this work as a class assignment and would like a marked copy returned to you, submit duplicate copies. The original can then be retained by your instructor.

When you submit your bibliography, include a short introduction to explain or define its subject. In it also include a list of the sources you used to find your references. This will allow your instructor to make constructive comments about your literature searching techniques.

THE ANNOTATED BIBLIOGRAPHY

Etymologically, a bibliography is simply a list of books. As used here, it is a list of the works consulted in preparing a research paper, or a list of sources of information on a given topic.

To cite is to refer to an item because it is the source of information incorporated in your report, or because it contains additional relevant material.

There are several kinds of annotations. Those you will prepare combine the first and last of the following sorts:

- *bibliographic annotation*—a succinct explanation or description of a cited item, prepared to guide the reader to worthwhile material
- *explanatory annotation*—an interpretation of a word, passage, or detail in a text for the purpose of clarifying what the author meant, sources used, variables in the interpretation, or variations among editions
- *analytical annotation*—fully describes and analyzes all matters relating to the work
- *evaluative annotation*—a description of the whole item, rather than its parts, which tells a reader about the item's contents— hence sometimes confused with an abstract

A working distinction can be made between abstract and annotation of the sort you'll use here. Like an abstract, an annotation summarizes a text; but unlike an abstract, it also characterizes (see Figure 11). The abstract tends to be longer than the annotation, primarily because it should touch on all relevant conclusions. An annotation can be considerably briefer because it merely indicates areas of content.

Annotation and citation styles vary. While no single form is easily designated "best," some are easier to scan than others.

Different bibliographies serve different purposes. One sort lists (and credits) the sources of an author's information; another lists comprehensively the books and articles of a single writer; a third kind lists works relevant to a specific subject area. The preparation of the last type, a subject bibliography, is your task now (this book's final exercise will call for preparation of the first kind). Subject bibliographies may be current (usually the case in science), retro-

63399. TIMMS, B. V. (Zool. Dep., Univ. Canterbury, Christchurch, N.Z.) PROC R SOC QUEENSL 0(90): 57–64. 1979. **The benthos of some lakes in northeastern Queensland, Australia.**—Lake Barrine has at least 25 macrobenthic species, Lake Eacham 19 and Lake Euramoo none; 3 floodplain lagoons on the lower Burdekin River average at least 9 spp. and 4 lagoons on the upper Burdekin and Lake Buchanan only 5 spp. These differences are influenced mainly by lake size, physicochemical stability and nature of the substrate. Chironomids, particularly *Chironomus nepeanensis* and *Procladius* sp. and the dipteran *Chaoborus* sp. were dominant in most lakes; in Barrine snails were also important. Most taxa are common components of the benthos of Australian lakes, but some are restricted to North Queensland. Biomass in all lakes was low (typically < 2 g/m²).

63400. LUEDTKE, NILE A. and MICHAEL L. BENDER. (Grad. Sch. Oceanogr., Univ. R.I., Narragansett Bay Campus, Kingston, R.I. 02881, USA.) ESTUARINE COASTAL MAR SCI 9(5): 643–652. 1979. **Tracer study of sediment-water interaction in estuaries.**—Rates of sediment bioturbation and advective exchange Narragansett Bay. Rhod experiments. The biologic 0.3 cm³/cm² per day) decrease in ²²Na concent animal pumping of watei coefficient of solid sedi distribution at the end o ⁵⁹Fe (which was quantiti experiment). The pore w similar to stable Mn pt radioisotopes added to the and 50% of Sr remained and < 1% of the Cd, Zi were terminated.

Physical Geology

551.1/.4(022)
HOLMES, A. Holmes' Principles of physical geology. 3rd ed., rev. by Doris L. Holmes. London, Nelson, 1978. [xv], 730p. illus., diagrs., geol. maps. £8.50.

First published 1944.

31 sections, each with selected references (eg, 5. Igneous rocks: volcanic and plutonic... 12. Volcanoes and their products (p.188-229. 47 illus. and diagrs.; 15 references)... 21. Ice Ages and their problems... 27. Magnetism, palaeomagnetism and drifting continents...). Analytical index. Very well illustrated. Excellent value; standard text.

Structural Geology

551.1(022)
DE SITTER, L.U. Structural geology. 2nd ed. New York, London, [etc.], McGraw-Hill, 1964. xii, 511p. diagrs. £16.50.

3 parts: 1. Theoretical structural geology (chapters 1-7) — 2. Comparative structural geology (ch. 8-24) — 3. Geotechnics (ch. 25-36). References, p. 503-30. 'It stands apart from most other books dealing with this subject in presenting facts and hypotheses with distinctive clarity' *(Geographical journal,* v. 123, pt. 2, June 1957, p. 256. on the 1st ed.). It makes great use of comparative aspects, whereas other books have a decided regional slant.

Noted: Billings, M.P. *Structural geology* (3rd ed.) (New York, Prentice-Hall, 1962. xv, 606p. illus, diagrs.).

Figure 11. Abstracts (left) and annotations (right) illustrated. (Sources are Biological Abstracts *and* Walford's 1973 Guide to Reference Material.*)*

spective, or a combination of both. If current, it will tend to emphasize periodical and journal literature, reports, research, and unpublished communications.

The following steps are recommended in preparing a subject bibliography:

1. Gain an overview of the project by examining the basic reference tools: almost all broad subject areas have basic guides (see Figure 12). Narrower guides and current and retrospective bibliographies treat the subfields of these subject areas. Therefore:

    a. Consult the general bibliographies for information on guides to the literature (see Figure 12).

    b. Search the general guides for the bibliographies of your specific field.

    c. In the specific bibliographies, note the references relevant to your subject area.

    d. Check any author lists that may be available. If author X is known to have written in your area of interest, search the appropriate indexes and abstracts under the author's name for more recent materials. *Science Citation Index* (*SCI*) (see Figure 6, p. 55) gives a list of authors whose scientific papers cite work by X, and *SCI*'s Source Index (see Figure 13) gives further information about the cited papers.

    e. Institutional reports that list publications, such as the *Annual Report of Argonne National Laboratories for Isotope Research*, can be very useful.

    f. Checking subject encyclopedias, handbooks, directories, and the like. Specific research guides, such as Thomas G. Kirk, Jr.'s, *Library Research Guide to Biology* (1978, Pierian Press, Ann Arbor, 84 pp.), can help at this point.

2. Determine the scope of your bibliography: will you use retrospective material, material in foreign languages, microforms, periodical articles, and manuscript material? Will the bibliography be comprehensive or selective? (Remember that your task here is to compile a comprehensive annotated bibliography of a restricted subject.)

3. Determine the arrangement whereby the material can be most easily located and understood. The usual methods of arrangement are: (a) alphabetical by author; (b) alphabetical by subject; (c) classified; and, (d) chronological.

CHRONOLOGY

Bond, John James. Handy-book of rules and tables for verifying dates with the Christian Era. London, Bell, 1875. 465p. (Repr.: N.Y., Russell & Russell, 1966)   **EB48**

> Subtitle: Giving an account of the chief eras, and systems used by various nations, with easy methods for determining the corresponding dates; with regnal years of English sovereigns from the Norman Conquest to the present time, 1066–1874.   CE11.B7

Cappelli, Adriano. Cronologia, cronografia e calendario perpetuo, dal principio dell' êra cristiana ai giorni nostri. Tavole cronologico-sincrone e quadri sinottici per verificare le date storiche. 2. ed. interamente rif. ed ampl. Milano, Hoepli, 1930. 566p. (Repr.: Milano, Hoepli, 1960)   **EB49**

> 1st ed. 1906.

Forty year English-Jewish calendar with corresponding English dates from 1960 till 2000; to be used also as a Yarzeit calendar. [n.p.], Greenfield, 1963. 1v., unpaged.   **EB50**

> Half-title: Hebrew-English calendar.

Freeman-Grenville, Greville Stewart Parker. The Muslim and Christian calendars, being tables for the conversion of Muslim and Christian dates from the Hijra to the year A.D. 2000. London, Oxford Univ. Pr., 1963. 87p.   **EB51**

> Includes examples to illustrate how the tables are to be used.
> CE59.F7

Ginzel, Friedrich Karl. Handbuch der mathematischen und technischen Chronologie, das Zeitrechnungswesen der Völker. Leipzig, J. C. Hinrichs, 1906–14. 3v.   **EB52**

> Contents: Bd.1, Zeitrechnung der Babylonier, Ägypter, Mohammedaner, Perser, Inder, Südostasiaten, Chinesen, Japaner und Zentralamerikaner; Bd.2, Zeitrechnung der Juden, der Naturvölker, der Römer und Griechen, sowie Nachträge zum 1. Bande; Bd.3, Zeitrechnung der Makedonier, Kleinasier und Syrer, der Germanen und Kelten, des Mittelalters, der Byzantiner (und Russen), Armenier, Kopten, Abessinier, Zeitrechnung der neueren Zeit, sowie Nachträge zu den drei Bänden. Each volume has its own index.
> CE11.G5

Master Reporting Company. A 200-year series of calendars, 1828–2028. N.Y., Master Reporting Co., [1932?] [16p.]
    EB53

Figure 12. A sample of text from Sheehy's 1976 Guide to Reference Books *published by the American Library Association.*

```
      see  BERGER JM      CR AC SCI B      270   733  70
      see  FESQUET J          "           271   773  70
ROIG JA
      BUDELLI R  MACADAR O  MONTI JM  HIPPOCAMPAL THETA
      RHYTHM IN RELATION WITH UNIT DISCHARGES IN SEPTUM
      AND HIPPOCAMPUS
        EEG CL NEUR      28   520  70  M  NO R     N5
      see  MACADAR O      PHYSL BEHAV      5  1443  70
ROIGAS H
      ZOELLNER E  JACOBASC G  SCHULTZE M  RAPOPORT S  (GE)
      REGULATORY FACTORS OF METHYLENE BLUE CATALYSIS IN
      ERYTHROCYTES
        EUR J BIOCH      12   24  70     32R        N1
ROIGDEVA CE
      see  BURGOS MH      AM J OBST G      108   565  70
ROIHA M
      see  ARELL A        PHYS KOND M      12    87  70
ROIKHEL VM
      see  ZEITLENO BA    B EX BIO R       67   171  69
ROINE K
      (SW) FREQUENCY OF RECURRENCE AMONG TREATED CASES
      OF PARESIS ANTE PARTUM AND PARESIS PUERPERALIS
        NORD VETMED      22   567  70     7R        N11
ROINE P
      see  KOIVISTO P     SUOM KEMIST      43   426  70
      see  PEKKARIN M     INT Z VITAM      40   555  70
ROINEL N
      (FR) APPLICATIONS OF MICROPROBE TO DOSAGE OF VERY
      SMALL VOLUMES OF BIOLOGICAL FLUIDS (LOWER VOLUMES
      AT 10 BILLION )
        J MICROSCOP       9   295  70  M   2R        3
ROINEL Y
      WINTER JM  (FR) NUCLEAR RELAXATION BY PARAMAGNETIC
      IMPURITIES DURING SELF-DIFFUSION
        J PHYSIQUE       31   351  70     14R        4
ROINESTA FA
      YALL I  VOLUTIN GRANULES IN ZOOGLOEA RAMIGERA
        APPL MICROB      19   973  70     13R        N6
ROING G
      see  SANTOS J       IEEE COMPUT      C 19  651  70
ROINISHV V
      see  BAUD R         PHYS LETT B      B 31  397  70
      see        "             "          B 31  401  70
      see        "             "          B 31  549  70
ROINISHV VN
      see  GRIGALAS MS    INSTR EXP R      1969  1559  69
      see  MANDZHAV ZS         "          1970    48  70
ROISENBE I
      MORTON WE  POPULATION STRUCTURE OF BLOOD GROUPS IN
      CENTRAL AMERICAN AND SOUTH AMERICAN INDIANS
        AM J P ANTH      32   373  70     25R        N3
ROISSARD JP
      see  MURAT J        PRESSE MED       78  2335  70
ROISTACH N
      STEELMAN DM  IN BETWEENS OF DDC DESIGN TO STARTUP
        IEEE IND AP      IGA5  766  69    NO R       N6
ROISTACH S
      see  POLAN M        J PROS DENT      24   335  70
ROITBERG MB
      NOVIK VA  GAVRILOV ND  CHARACTERISTIC FEATURES OF
      PYROELECTRIC EFFECT AND ELECTRICAL CONDUCTIVITY IN
      SINGLE CRYSTALS OF LINBO3 IN RANGE 70-250 DEGREES C
        SOV PH CR R      14   814  70  M  NO R       N5
ROITBERG YA
      (RS) THEOREM OF HOMEOMORPHISMS FOR GENERAL
      ELLIPTIC BOUNDARY VALUE PROBLEMS WITH BOUNDARY
      CONDITIONS NOT BEING NORMAL
        DAN SSSR        191  1228  70     18R        N6
      SHEFTEL ZG  (RS) ON A CLASS OF GENERAL NONLOCAL
      ELLIPTIC PROBLEMS
        DAN SSSR        192   511  70     7R         N1
ROITENBE EY
      (RS) ON OBSERVABILITY OF SOLUTIONS OF NONLINEAR
      DIFFERENTIAL EQUATIONS IN HILBERT SPACE
        DAN SSSR        192   746  70     4R         N4
ROITENBE YY
      OBSERVABILITY OF NONLINEAR SYSTEMS
        SIAM J CONT       8   338  70     4R         N3
ROITENBU DI
      see  GEMBARZH GV    OPT SPECT R      28   593  70
ROITHMAY CM
      AIRBORNE LOW-LIGHT SENSOR DETECTS LUMINESCING FISH
      SCHOOLS AT NIGHT
        COMMER FISH      32    42  70     22R        N12
      see  RIVAS LR       COPEIA           1970   771  70
ROITMAN D
      JONES WB  SHEFFIEL LT  COMPARISON OF SUBMAXIMAL
      EXERCISE ECG TEST WITH CORONARY CINEANGIOCARDIOGRAM
        ANN INT MED      72   641  70     22R        N5
      JONES WB  SHEFFIEL LT  COMPARISON OF SUBMAXIMAL
      EXERCISE ECG TEST WITH CORONARY CINEANGIOCARDIOGRAM
        ANN INT MED      72   641  70     22R        N5
      see  JACKSON DH     CIRCULATION      42  1154  70
ROITMAN GP
      CHIBISOV AK  KARYAKIN AV  (RS) PHOTOOXIDATION OF
      THIAZINE DYES WITH PARA-BENZOQUINONE UNDER PULSED
      EXCITATION
        DAN SSSR        194  1104  70     6R         N5
      see  CHIBISOV AK    LAN SSS FIZ      34  1288  70
ROITMAN J
      see  PITTMAN AG     J POL SCI B       8   873  70
ROITMAN LI
      see  LOMONOSO SA    ZH ANAL KH       25  1170  70
ROITSHTE LN
      MURAVICH  ELTSOV AV  SYNTHETIC ANALOGS OF KINETIN

ROJAS E
      TAYLOR RE  CALCIUM INFLUXES IN PERFUSED SQUID GIANT
      AXONS DURING VOLTAGE CLAMP
        J PHYSL LON      210  P135  70  M   2R        2
      BEZANILL F  TAYLOR RE  DEMONSTRATION OF SODIUM AND
      POTASSIUM CONDUCTANCE CHANGES DURING A NERVE
      ACTION POTENTIAL
        NATURE          225   747  70     4R  N5234
      see  ATWATER I      J PHYSL LON      211   753  70
      see  BEZANILL F     J GEN PHYSL       55   143  70
      see        "        J PHYSL LON      207   151  70
      see        "             "          211   729  70
      see  COHEN LB       J PHYSL PAR       62   143  70
      see  VEGA P         ARCH BIOL M        6  R 33  69
ROJAS F
      see  ROMERO T       CIRCULATION       42  1192  70
ROJAS G
      see  ASENJO A       REV NEUROL       121   581  69
ROJAS L
      SOELDNER JS  GLEASON RE  KAHN CB  MARBLE A
      OFFSPRING OF 2 DIABETIC PARENTS  DIFFERENTIAL SERUM
      INSULIN RESPONSES TO INTRAVENOUS GLUCOSE AND
      TOLBUTAMIDE
        J CLIN END       79  1569  69     38R       N12
      see  KASHYAP ML     CAN MED A J      102  1165  70
ROJAS LL
      see  COSTA RP       RAD DIAGN         10   365  69
ROJAS LR
      see  COSTA RP       RAD DIAGN         11   123  70
ROJAS M
      see  FARIAS G       ARCH BIOL M        6  R 13  69
ROJAS RH
      LANGE R  PSEUDOANEURYSM OF SPLENIC ARTERY
        J AM MED A       213   627  70  L  2R         4
      see  ROSENBERG JM   AM J HOSP P       27   753  70
ROJAS SW
      LUNG AB  WINODEGU RV  EFFECTS OF PERUVIAN ANCHOVY
      (ENGRAULIS RINGENS) MEAL SUPPLEMENTED WITH
      SANTOQUIN ON GROWTH AND FISHY FLAVOR OF BROILERS
        POULTRY SCI      48  2045  69     23R        N6
ROJAS WR
      (SP) AUTORADIOGRAPHIC STUDY OF ERITHROIDCELLS OF
      BONE MARROW OF NORMAL CALVES AND WITH IN VITRO
      PORPHYROSIS
        ARCH BIOL M        6  R 28  69  M  NO R      1-3
ROJASCOR RR
      see  CUNNINGHAW     EXPERIENTIA       26    13  70
ROJASLOP RM
      see  ROSADO  JA     AN QUIMICA        66   339  70
ROJASMIR A
      see  LEBRIGAN H     PRESSE MED       -78  1475  70
ROJASRAM JA
      TAUBER ES  PARADOXICAL SLEEP IN 2 SPECIES OF AVIAN
      PREDATOR (FALCONIFORMES)
        SCIENCE         167  1754  70     10R  N1976
      see  DRUCKERC RR    BRAIN RES         23   269  70
ROJEK N
      ERROR IN RADIATION COUNTING
        J NUCL MED       11   413  70  M  NO R       N6
ROJEY A
      see  LENOIR JY      SEPARAT SCI        5   545  70
ROJKIND M
      DIAZDELE L  COLLAGEN BIOSYNTHESIS IN CIRRHOTIC RAT
      LIVER SLICES A REGULATORY MECHANISM
        BIOC BIOP A      217   512  70     38R         2
      see  KERSHENO D     J CLIN INV        49  2246  70
ROJKOV V
      SOME ASPECTS OF NUCLEAR DEVELOPMENT IN USSR
        J BR NUCL E        9   258  70  M  NO R        4
ROJO M
      EEG IN PSYCHOPATHOLOGY
        EEG CL NEUR       29    98  70  M  NO R        1
ROJOORTE JM
      GRANGER P  BOUCHER R  GENEST J  STUDIES ON
      DISTRIBUTION OF JGI IN RENAL CORTEX OF DOGS AND
      BEAVERS
        NEPHRON           7    61  70     12R        N1
      GENEST J  (FR) INDEX OF HISTOCHEMICAL ACTIVITY OF
      GLUCOSE 6-PHOSPHATE DEHYDROGENASE IN MACULA DENSA
      (MD) AND ITS DISTRIBUTION IN RENAL CORTEX OF RAT
        PATH BIOL        18   595  70     14R   11-14
      see  HAYDUK K       CAN J PHYSL       48   463  70
      see        "        P SOC EXP M      135   271  70
      see  HORKY K        AM J PHYSL       219   387  70
      see  NAWAR T        ANN INT MED       72   529  70
      see  RODRIGUE J     UN MED CAN        99   329  70
ROKA L
      see  HAAS H         Z KLIN CHEM        8   218  70
      see  HEINRICH D     KLIN WOCH         48   235  70
ROKACHEV OP
      see  VOLFSON SA     DAN SSSR         194  1111  70
ROKEACH M
      HOMANT R  PENNER L  A VALUE ANALYSIS OF DISPUTED
      FEDERALIST PAPERS
        J PERS SOC       16   245  70     7R         N2
      FAITH HOPE BIGOTRY
        PSYCHOL TOD        3    33  70     6R        N11
ROKERYA MS
      see  IQBAL M        J APPL MECH       37   931  70
ROKHLENK AV
      LAVRENKO VA  YASINETS VA  (RS) A METHOD FOR
      MEASUREMENT OF ATOM RECOMBINATION COEFFICIENTS ON
      SURFACE BY MEANS OF ELECTRON PARAMAGNETIC
      RESONANCE
        DAN SSSR        191  1327  70     2R         N6
```

Figure 13. A sample of text from SCI's *Source Index.*

4. Choose a format for your entries. The usual elements for bibliographic citation and attribution include: author (use of given name, initials, and internal punctuation should mirror the cited author's use); title; edition; imprint (place, publisher, date); collation (paging, illustrations, etc.); and, possibly, series note. Your entries must be consistent and complete so that the others can locate exactly the works you cite.

5. In your annotations, as your readings distinguish fact, opinion, conclusion, judgment, inference, and the like.

6. Use index cards to collect your citations: they are easy to rearrange.

Perusal of a dozen journals in your field of interest will convince you that there is no universal standard for bibliographic citation. Most professional journals specify that a particular citing style be followed. Useful citations, however, include all the information required for a reader to recognize and find the work cited. The scheme given here (see Figure 14) for citing bibliographical elements (whether or not annotated) is one of many conventional forms. Avoid confusion for yourself, authors, editors, reviewers, and publishers by using common sense: find out whether a particular citation style is required on the job you're doing. Most journals require a specific style, so check the publisher's style book if there is one. If there is no style book, study examples in the journal itself. If all else fails, devise a style suitable to the subject matter and use it consistently. Turabian's *A manual for writers of term papers, theses, and dissertations* contains a standard guide for citations.

Consistency of format is one hallmark of good bibliography (sometimes called a *references cited* section). Citations in a research paper ordinarily omit a work's dimensions, weight, and price. Citations are generally given alphabetically, by first author's last name; when several works by the same author are cited, they are listed chronologically. If several works by the same author(s) were published in the same year, they are sequenced by means of a lowercase alphabet. Thus, if two papers written in 1975 and one in 1976 by Jones would be referred to, the text citation could read: Jones (1975a, 1975b, 1976). Avoiding abbreviation simplifies your task, precludes confusion for your reader, and takes little extra space.

This section would be incomplete without a short mention of plagiarism and copyright laws. Plagiarism is the unacknowledged use of someone else's work. Proper citations acknowledge the source of ideas not your own. With more than a quarter million[1] scientific

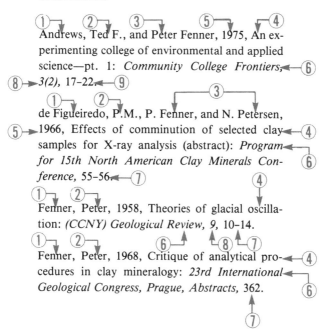

JOURNAL ARTICLES AND ABSTRACTS

Andrews, Ted F., and Peter Fenner, 1975, An experimenting college of environmental and applied science—pt. 1: *Community College Frontiers,* *3(2),* 17–22.

de Figueiredo, P.M., P. Fenner, and N. Petersen, 1966, Effects of comminution of selected clay samples for X-ray analysis (abstract): *Program for 15th North American Clay Minerals Conference,* 55–56.

Fenner, Peter, 1958, Theories of glacial oscillation: *(CCNY) Geological Review, 9,* 10–14.

Fenner, Peter, 1968, Critique of analytical procedures in clay mineralogy: *23rd International Geological Congress, Prague, Abstracts,* 362.

Key: **1.** Last name of first author. **2.** Given name or initials (per article's title page). **3.** Other authors (names *not* inverted). **4.** Title with (only initial word capped). **5.** Year of publication. **6.** Journal title. **7.** Page span. **8.** Vol. number (issue number).

Figure 14. A suitable citation scheme.

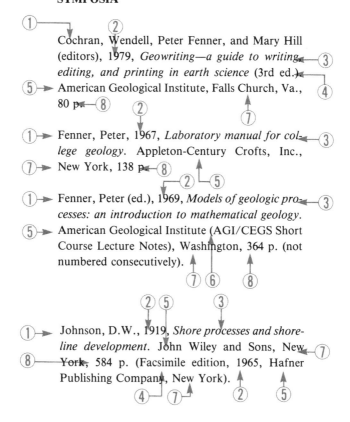

BOOKS AND COMPLETE SYMPOSIA

Cochran, Wendell, Peter Fenner, and Mary Hill (editors), 1979, *Geowriting—a guide to writing, editing, and printing in earth science* (3rd ed.). American Geological Institute, Falls Church, Va., 80 p.

Fenner, Peter, 1967, *Laboratory manual for college geology.* Appleton-Century Crofts, Inc., New York, 138 p.

Fenner, Peter (ed.), 1969, *Models of geologic processes: an introduction to mathematical geology.* American Geological Institute (AGI/CEGS Short Course Lecture Notes), Washington, 364 p. (not numbered consecutively).

Johnson, D.W., 1919, *Shore processes and shoreline development.* John Wiley and Sons, New York, 584 p. (Facsimile edition, 1965, Hafner Publishing Company, New York).

Key: 1. Name of single or multiple authors (or editors). **2.** Year of publication. **3.** Book title. **4.** Edition (if not first). **5.** Publisher. **6.** Series name. **7.** Place of publication. **8.** Page span.

Figure 14 (continued).

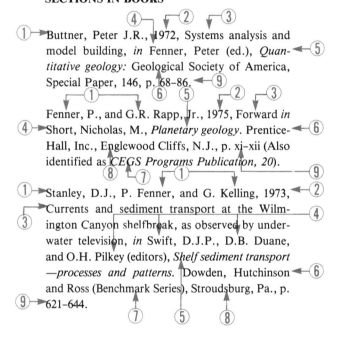

ARTICLES OR ABSTRACTS IN SYMPOSIA OR OTHER COLLECTIONS, INCLUDING SECTIONS IN BOOKS

Buttner, Peter J.R., 1972, Systems analysis and model building, *in* Fenner, Peter (ed.), *Quantitative geology:* Geological Society of America, Special Paper, 146, p. 68–86.

Fenner, P., and G.R. Rapp, Jr., 1975, Forward *in* Short, Nicholas, M., *Planetary geology.* Prentice-Hall, Inc., Englewood Cliffs, N.J., p. xi–xii (Also identified as *CEGS Programs Publication, 20*).

Stanley, D.J., P. Fenner, and G. Kelling, 1973, Currents and sediment transport at the Wilmington Canyon shelfbreak, as observed by underwater television, *in* Swift, D.J.P., D.B. Duane, and O.H. Pilkey (editors), *Shelf sediment transport —processes and patterns.* Dowden, Hutchinson and Ross (Benchmark Series), Stroudsburg, Pa., p. 621–644.

Key: 1. Name of authors (or editors). 2. Year of publication. 3. Title of individual paper. 4. Name of author or editor of book as a whole. 5. Title of symposium or collection. 6. Publisher (or journal citation). 7. Series title (if needed). 8. Place of publication. 9. Page span of article or abstract.

Figure 14 (continued).

THESES AND
DISSERTATIONS

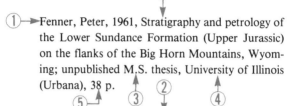

②

①—▶Fenner, Peter, 1961, Stratigraphy and petrology of
the Lower Sundance Formation (Upper Jurassic)
on the flanks of the Big Horn Mountains, Wyom-
ing; unpublished M.S. thesis, University of Illinois
(Urbana), 38 p.

⑤   ③   ②   ④

①—▶Fenner, Peter, 1963, Variations in mineralogy and
trace elements, Esopus Formation, Kingston, New
York; Ph.D. dissertation, University of Illinois
(Urbana), 83 p.◀—⑤

③   ④

Key: 1. Name of author. 2. Title of thesis. 3. Degree for
which thesis was written. 4. Institution. 5. Page span.

Figure 14 (continued).

and technical articles being added to the formal literature every year it is probable that some of your ideas have already been expressed elsewhere. Authors have an obligation to search the literature and to know what is and what isn't original with them—particularly in research areas.

Thus, when you write a technical paper you must identify information you have garnered from other sources, and you must identify the sources themselves. This is an accountability that sets professionals apart. It assures that credit is given where it is due.

You should also be aware of the impact of copyright law on users of the literature. This law can affect you whether you intend to quote or copy materials for yourself, co-workers, other students, or students in your classroom.

The new copyright law was accompanied by a text ("Agreement on guidelines for classroom copying in not-for profit educational institutions," *House Report* 94-1476, pp. 68–70) agreed upon by representatives of educational organizations, authors, and publishers; its purpose was to set minimum standards for fair use of protected materials. It permits researchers to make single copies of reasonable length for their own scholarly purposes or as preparation for teaching. More severe restrictions govern the number of copies teachers may make for use in the classroom. Ethical and professional as well as legal standards dictate: attribute, cite, and when others' work is used extensively, obtain permission before using.[2] If needed references are not in your library, use a larger regional or institutional library, or ask your librarian whether interlibrary loans can be arranged to meet your needs.

Figure 15 shows a cover sheet we have used with our students. It has helped us to manage this assignment responsibly.

DATA COMPILATION AND ATTRIBUTION

The object of scientific research and publication is to expand one's store of knowledge and communicate that knowledge to the science community and other publics. This exercise requires you to undertake a project of basic library research. Select a topic relevant to your needs and interests, so that the product you develop here will contribute to your own professional growth or private endeavors. Your compilation of data must be original.

Decide on your subject area and on the form your data presentation will take—e.g., tables, graphs, charts, an essay, and so forth. Figure 16 illustrates one method for presenting data. (With your presentation, of course, you will include full bibliographic details for the sources used.)

CONTRACT 3.1

Student: _____

Subject chosen for
annotated bibliography: _____
_____
_____
_____
_____

Subject matter expert, for
evaluation assistance: _____
(affiliation address/phone): _____
_____
_____

(note: subject matter expert should be agreed upon by student and instructor)

Anticipated completion date: _____

Sources used to find references: _____
_____
_____

Subject approval signature: _____

Completion approval date: _____

Comments:

Figure 15. See text.

Table 5. Trace element abundances from other sources

	Fresh-water Shales	Marine Shales	Undifferentiated Shales	Limestones and Dolomites	Limestones and Sandstones	Sandstones	Greywackes and Siltstones	Common Sedimentary Rocks	References
B			20–310	1.5–3	56	9–31	35–170	1.5–3.0	Go, Gr, Me, Mr, R, We, Wh
Ba	210–950	280–550	300–2240	120	20–200	100–500		20–2240	D, Gr, K, Mr, P, R, We
Be	8–20	5.5–15	1–6	0–1		0–2		0–20	D, Go, Gr, K, Mr, P, R
Ca			2.2–4.2	30.4		3.95		2.2–30.4	Gr, R
Co			1–68	0–2	10	0–50	8–22	0–250	C, Go, Gr, K, Me, Mr, P, R, We, Wh, Y
Cr	35–185	35–90	10–400	5–20.2	24	10–100	140	10–400	D, Go, Gr, K, Mr, P, R, We, Wh
Cu	38–90	58–100	0–1000	2–20	24	10–200	33–68	0–1000	D, Go, Gr, K, Me, Mr, P, R, We, Wh
Ga			5–100	3.7	tr–14	5–10	14–20	tr–100	B, F, Go, Gr, K, Me, P, R, We, Wh
Ge	1.7–7					1–3		1–7	B, E, F, Go, Gr, K, P, R
La			17–18.3			<1		<1–18.3	Gr, P, R
Li			2–300	2–26		7–29		2–300	Go, Gr, H, K, Mr, P, R
Mn	175–2800	180–3800	160–7600	385		tr–77.5	600	tr–7600	D, Go, Gr, P, R, We, Wh
Ni	15–40	20–100	2–152	0–22		0–50	43–54	0–152	D, Go, Gr, K, Me, Mr, P, R, Wh
Pb	10–80	12–50	9–125	5–10	5–10	9–40		5–125	D, Go, Gr, K, P, R, We
Rb			63–700	0–100	23	270–273		0–700	Gr, K, R
Sc			0–30	0		0.7–1		0–30	Gr, K, Me, P, R, We
Sn	1–10	1–5	40				8–20	1–40	D, Go, K, R
Sr	180–550	300–550	14–1300	400–800	10–52	26–45	260	14–1300	D, Gr, K, Mr, P, R, We
V	30–80	20–70	10–300	2–20		10–60	67–85	2–300	D, Go, Gr, K, Me, Mr, P, R, We, Wh
Y			1.6–28.1	0	1–6	4		0–28.1	F, Gr, P, R
Zn			19–1000	4–50		5–20		4–1000	Go, Gr, K, P, R
Zr			37–1000				400	37–1000	Gr, K, Mr, P, R, We, Wh

Some of these values are from compilations of data from the literature and others are from small-scale studies. The reference abbreviations are : B = BURTON and others, 1959; C = CARR and TUREKIAN, 1961; D = DEGENS and others, 1957; E = EL WARDANI, 1957; F = FLEISCHER, 1955, Go = GOLDSCHMIDT, 1954; Gr = GREEN, 1959; H = HORSTMAN, 1957; K = KRAUSKOPF, 1955; Me = MOORE, 1963; Mr = MOHR, 1959; P = PETTIJOHN, 1963; R = RANKAMA and SAHAMA, 1950; We = WEBER, 1961, Wh = WHITE, 1959 and Y = YOUNG, 1967. All values are in parts per million except Ca, in per cent. Some values are only approximate.

Figure 16. Example of data compilation.

CONTRACT 3.2

Student: _____

Subject chosen for data
compilation & bibliography: _____
_____
_____
_____

Form that data will take: _____
_____

Subject matter expert, for
evaluation assistance: _____

(affiliation address/phone): _____
_____
_____

(note: subject matter expert should be agreed upon by student and instructor)

Anticipated completion date: _____

Sources used to find references: _____
_____
_____

Did you do original research to complete this
bibliography? _____

Subject approval signature: _____

Completion approval date: _____

Comments:

Figure 17. See text.

Figure 17 shows the cover sheet we use with our students. We require that the compiler's subject and plan be approved before work is started.

Compile and develop the data, giving references in full. It is permissible (though not required) that some of the data included in your work be original, previously unreported data from your own studies. Unless format prevents it, type your assignment; in any event, type the references cited in the same format as used for your annotated bibliography. Remember—as before—if this is to be used as classwork, submit a copy of your contract with your work. (Also, if you want the project returned, submit the original and a duplicate.) All cited references must be in the bibliography; in your bibliography cite only material you actually used.

Finally, should your work carry sufficient new information—or old information newly arranged—to be considered for wider dissemination, where would you go to accomplish that goal? Good luck!

NOTES

1. National Science Board data for 1974–1977.

2. Given that legal actions have already been taken against parties accused of illegal photocopying, and as a matter of interest to some readers of this book, the "Guidelines" for copying from books and periodicals, referred to above, are reproduced here:

Guidelines

I. Single Copying for Teachers

A single copy may be made of any of the following by or for a teacher at his or her individual request for his or her scholarly research or use in teaching or preparation to teach a class:

A. A chapter from a book;

B. An article from a periodical or newspaper;

C. A short story, short essay or short poem, whether or not from a collective work;

D. A chart, graph, diagram, drawing, cartoon or picture from a book, periodical, or newspaper.

II. Multiple Copies for Classroom Use

Multiple copies (not to exceed in any event more than one copy per pupil in a course) may be made by or for the teacher giving the course for classroom use or discussion, provided that:

A. The copying meets the tests of brevity and spontaneity as defined below; and

B. Meets the cumulative effective test as defined below; and,

C. Each copy includes a notice of copyright.

Definitions

Brevity

(i) Poetry: (a) A complete poem if less than 250 words and if printed on not more than two pages, or (b) from a longer poem, an excerpt of not more than 250 words.

(ii) Prose: (a) Either a complete article, story or essay of less than 2,500 words, or (b) an excerpt from any prose work of not more than 1,000 words or 10 percent of the work, whichever is less, but in any event a minimum of 500 words.

[Each of the numerical limits stated in *i* and *ii* above may be expanded to permit the completion of an unfinished line of a poem or of an unfinished prose paragraph.]

(*iii*) Illustration: One chart, graph, diagram, drawing, cartoon or picture per book or per periodical issue.

(*iv*) "Special" works: Certain works in poetry, prose or in "poetic prose" which often combine language with illustrations and which are intended sometimes for children and at other times for a more general audience fall short of 2,500 words in their entirety. Paragraph *ii* above notwithstanding, such "special works" may not be reproduced in their entirety; however, an excerpt comprising not more than two of the published pages of such special work and containing not more than 10 percent of the words found in the text thereof, may be reproduced.

Spontaneity

(*i*) The copying is at the instance and inspiration of the individual teacher, and

(*ii*) The inspiration and decision to use the work and the moment of its use for maximum teaching effectiveness are so close in time that it would be unreasonable to expect a timely reply to a request for permission.

Cumulative Effect

(*i*) The copying of the material is for only one course in the school in which the copies are made.

(*ii*) Not more than one short poem, article, story, essay or two excerpts may be copied from the same author, nor more than three from the same collective work or periodical volume during one class term.

(*iii*) There shall not be more than nine instances of such multiple copying for one course during one class term.

[The limitations stated in *ii* and *iii* above shall not apply to current news periodicals and newspapers and current news sections of other periodicals.]

III. Prohibitions as to I and II Above

Notwithstanding any of the above, the following shall be prohibited:

A. Copying shall not be used to create or to replace or substitute for anthologies, compilations or collective works. Such replacement or substitution may occur whether copies of various works or excerpts therefrom are accumulated or reproduced and used separately.

B. There shall be no copying of or from works intended to be "consumable" in the course of study or of teaching. These include workbooks, exercises, standardized tests and test booklets and answer sheets and like consumable material.

C. Copying shall not:
(a) substitute for the purchase of books, publishers' reprints or periodicals;
(b) be directed by higher authority;
(c) be repeated with respect to the same item by the same teacher from term to term.

D. No charge shall be made to the student beyond the actual cost of the photocopying.

Index

AACR2, 134
ABI, 89
Abstract journals, 138
Abstracting serials, 41, 85
Abstracts, 20, 21, 53
Abstracts journal, 21, 33
Added entries, 14
Ainsworth, T. D., ix
Alexander The Great, 127
Alexandria, 127
Alphabetization, 1
Ambrosian Library, 129
American Statistics Index, 65
American Geological Institute, 88, 138
American Library Association, 129
American Men and Women of Science, 44
Analytical annotation, 153
Anglo-American Catalog Rules, 134
Annals, 32
Annotated bibliography, 152
Annual report of Argonne Natl. Labs. for isotope resch., 155
Applied Science and Technology Index, 45, 51–52
Aramaeans, 126
Archival holdings, 138
Art slides, 22
ASCA, 88
Ascatopics, 88
ASI, 65
Assurbanipal, 125
Atlases, 21, 41, 46, 81
Attribution, 163
Austrian Royal Library, 129
Author, 22
Author-title cards, 44
Author-title catalog, 2
Author-title headings, 2
Author's name, 12
Author's profession, 45
Author's year of birth, 12

Author's year of death, 12
Automated subject citation alert, 88

Babylonia, 125
Bacon, Sir Francis, 39
Behistun inscription, 125
Beveridge, W. I. B., 39, 68
Bible, 126, 128, 150
Bibliographic annotation, 153
Bibliographic citations, 159
Bibliographic Retrieval Services, Inc., 88
Bibliographies, 21, 41, 83, 138, 152
Bibliography entry format, 158
Bibliography of Agriculture, 67
Bibliography to Earth Science Bibliographies, 47
Bibliotheque Nationale de Paris, 129
Biographies, 41, 44–45
Biographies—current, 76
Biographies—deceased, 76
Biographies—persons of all times, 76
Biological Abstracts, 59, 62, 154
Biological Abstracts/RRM, 59
Biosis, 59
Birthdates, 44
Bonn, G. S., 132–36
Book description, 12
Books in Print, 47
Bowen, D. H. M., 31
Branscomb, L., 140–142, 150
British Museum Library, 129
BRS, 88
Bureau of Mines, 67
Burke, R., ix

Cain, 89
Call number, 12
Cambridge University Library, 129
Canaanite script, 126
Card automated reproduction demand system, 133
Card catalog, 14, 20, 44

Composed in Phototype Century
Schoolbook and Phototype Helvetica
by Trend Western Technical
Corporation. Printed Offset by
Malloy Lithographing Inc., Ann
Arbor, Michigan, on sixty pound
Gladfelter B-31 Wove Finish

Subject	LC	Decimal
American	PS	810
German	PT	830
Science	Q	500
Mathematics	QA	510
Computers	QA 76	519.4
Algebra	QA 150	512
Probability	QA 273	519.2
Geometry	QA 440	516
Analytic Mechanics	QA 801	516.3
Astronomy	QB	520
Geodesy	QB 275	526.1
Cosmogeny	QB 981	523.12
Physics	QC	530
Weights & Measures	QC 81	351.821
Atomic Physics	QC 170	539.7
Acoustics	QC 221	729.29
Heat	QC 251	536
Optics	QC 350	621.388
Radiation Physics	QC 474	539.2
Electricity & Magnetism	QC 501	537
Nuclear & Particle Physics	QC 770	539.74
Geophysics	QC 801	551
Geomagnetism	QC 811	523.018
Meteorology	QC 851	551.5
Chemistry	QD	540
Analytical Chemistry	QD 71	543
Inorganic Chemistry	QD 146	546
Organic Chemistry	QD 241	547
Physical & Theoretical Chemistry	QD 450	541.3
Crystallography	QD 901	548.83
Geology	QE	550
Mineralogy	QE 351	549
Petrology	QE 420	552
Dynamic & Structural Geology	QE 500	551.8
Stratigraphy	QE 640	551.7
Paleontology	QE 701	560
Natural History	QH	500
Microscopy	QH 201	502.82
Biology (General)	QH 301	574
Evolution	QH 359	575
Genetics	QH 426	575.1
Ecology	QH 540	574.5
Cytology	QH 573	574.87

continued from front end papers